This book belongs to

_____

...a woman with a high calling from God.

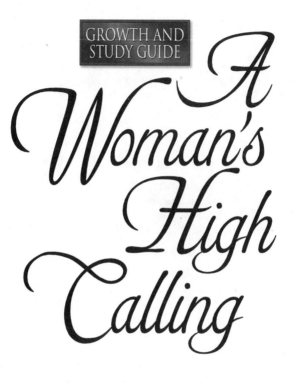

GROWTH AND STUDY GUIDE

A Woman's High Calling

Elizabeth George

HARVEST HOUSE PUBLISHERS
Eugene, Oregon 97402

Cover design by Terry Dugan and Associates, Minneapolis, Minnesota

∽ Acknowledgment ∽

As always, thank you to my dear husband, Jim George, M.Div., Th.M., for your able assistance, guidance, suggestions, and loving encouragement on this project.

Contents

A Word of Welcome

Please let me welcome you to this fun (and stretching!) growth and study guide for women like you who want to know—and answer—God's high callings to you as a Christian woman. I know you will be blessed to learn about the "Ten Essentials for Godly Living" as spelled out for us in Titus 2:3-5. In fact, they should be life-changing. Why? Because in this one tiny passage in the Bible, God sets forth two lifetime goals for you and me and every woman who is a Christian:

Learning about *a woman's high calling,* and

Teaching others about *a woman's high calling.*

A Word of Instruction

The exercises in this study guide should be easy to follow and to do. You'll need your copy of the book *A Woman's High Calling,* and your Bible, a pen, a dictionary, and a heart ready to grow. In each lesson you'll be asked to:

§ Read the corresponding chapter from *A Woman's High Calling.*

§ Answer the questions designed to guide you to greater growth.

§ Write out your own "Prayer for Godly Living."

A Word for Your Group

Of course, you can grow (volumes!) as you work your way, alone, through these truths from God's Word and apply them to your heart and home. But I urge you to share the journey with other women. A group, no matter how small or large, offers personal care and interest. There is sharing. There are sisters-in-Christ to pray for you. There is the mutual exchange of experiences. There is account-ability. And, yes there is peer pressure...which always helps us to get our lessons done! And there is sweet, sweet encouragement as together you stimulate one another to greater love and greater works of love (Hebrews 10:24).

An added benefit, too, is that you will be fulfilling one of the lifetime goals God sets for you—you will be *learning* the good things of Titus 2:3-5.

And if you are leading this study, you'll be fulfilling the other lifetime goal God sets for you—you will be *teaching* the good things of Titus 2:3-5 to others. (To aid the woman who is guided by God to lead a group, I've included a section in the back of this growth and study book called "Leading a Bible Study Discussion Group.")

A Word of Encouragement

What a wonderful surprise awaits you as you open up this book that is focused on (and hopefully opens up the meaning of!) just three verses of the Bible—Titus 2:3-5. These sacred scriptures contain ten of God's high callings to you as a Christian woman—ten essentials for godly living! And they are truly essentials that can easily turn your life around! As I wrote in the book *A Woman's High Calling,*

> Every woman desires peace and order in her
> life. Every woman would love to exchange

failure and frustration for a sure formula for success. Every woman would love to replace a life of survival with a life of meaningful accomplishment. And every women would love to give up the confusion she so easily gives in to for a lifetime characterized by simplicity and stability.[1]

Do these sound like your heart cries, my friend? Every woman of God desires to live out a high and sacred mission on earth...and there can be no higher nor more sacred mission on earth than to answer God's high calling to you to spend your days serving Him, serving others, and living a godly life.

A Word of Challenge

Dear one, it's been said that we are living in a post-Christian era. The vast majority of people in our neighborhoods, at our work, and in the marketplace have very little knowledge of the Bible and its teachings. They have little or no understanding of who Jesus Christ is, not to mention His transforming power.

What role can you, as one Christian woman, play in helping a lost world understand the reality of our risen Savior? How can you expose those around you to the truths of God's message of salvation as revealed in the Bible?

In these three verses, Titus 2:3-5, God gives direction for all women for all times—including you!—on how to live a godly life and how to be a godly influence on others. By pursuing the ten essentials for godly living offered to you here, your family will be blessed. Christ will be exemplified. God will be honored. And you will have answered "a woman's high calling" from Him!

Chapter One

*ssential

A Woman's High Calling to Godliness

*"the older women [are to] be
reverent in behavior"*
—TITUS 2:3

Begin this lesson by reading chapter 1, "A Woman's High Calling to Godliness," in your personal copy of *A Woman's High Calling*. Note here any new truths or challenges that stand out to you.

I hope you enjoyed reading about Canterbury Cathedral and its worshipful environment. Can you remember a place that inspired a spirit of worship in your soul? Describe that place and reflect on its spiritual impact on your thoughts toward God.

God's High Calling to Godliness

Read Titus 2:1-6 and note the groups that made up the churches on the island of Crete. Then write out Paul's instructions to each group.

*older men: be temperate, worthy of respect,
self controlled & sound in faith in love
+ endurance
older women: be reverent in way they live
not to be slanders or addicted to much wine
but teach what is good.
Train younger women to love their husbands
+ children - to be self controlled &
purely, be busy at home to be kind
to their husbands.*

Learning About Godliness

Having read the chapter on godliness, write out in your own
words your understanding of the phrase "reverent in behavior."

God strict in behavior

In 1 Timothy 2:9-15, the apostle Paul addressed this same
essential for godliness in the women of the church at Ephesus. How were the women in the church to dress (verse 9)?

modestly with decency + propriety.

And why (verse 10)?

*Good deeds appropriate for women
who profess to worship God.*

What ministry was to preoccupy these Christian women
(verse 10)?

Worship God

How were they to behave in the church service
(verses 11-12)?

Silent & full of submission.

What two reasons did Paul give for this behavior (verses 13-14)? *Adam formed 1st, Adam was not the one deceived it was the woman who was deceived + became a sinner.*

How does 1 Timothy 2:9-15 add to your understanding of "reverent in behavior"? *Women will be saved if they continue in faith, love + holiness with propriety.*

Living Out Godliness

Evaluate your life in the following areas that call for (and indicate) godliness, and list any changes you need to make in order to pursue godliness.

❧ Conduct *control temper + tongue*

❧ Speech

❧ Thought life

Holiness does not consist in mystic speculations, enthusiastic fervors, or uncommanded austerities; *it consists in thinking as God thinks and willing as God wills.*[2]

Godliness Lived Out in Another

Anna was a woman who loved God and who lived out that love in a lifestyle of godliness. Fill in the description of Anna's life from Luke 2:36-38:

Occupation— *prophetess*

Heritage— *tribe of Asher.*

Marital status— *married*

Age— *84*

Residence— *temple*

Daily duties— *worshiped nite + day fasting + praying.*

Attitude toward life— *giving thanks to God.*

Write out how each of these following facts about Anna's lifestyle shows a spirit of godliness.

§   She lived her life in the temple. *worshipping and praising God.*

§   She lived her life in prayer and fasting.
at temple

§   She lived her life in anticipation of the Savior.
waiting to see the savior

Before we move on, let's pause and give extra attention to the spiritual practices of prayer and fasting. Fasting was a form of worship practiced in biblical times, and is a form of worship that enhances our spiritual life today. In Anna's case, fasting and prayer were two ways she focused her attention on the things of God. Fasting was (and is) also used to beseech God in specific issues of vital importance. Look up the following passages and note the reason for each occasion for fasting.

2 Samuel 12:16— *he pleaded with God for the child,*

Nehemiah 1:4— *Mourned-Jerusalem broke down.*

Esther 4:16— *fast for Mordecai*

Acts 13:2— *Set apart Barnabas & Saul for the work I have called them*

In my book *Loving God with All Your Mind* I described how I was faced with a specific issue that only God could resolve. It was during the Desert Storm military crisis in Kuwait. At that time my husband Jim was in the Army Reserves. Our days found us waiting to see whether he was going to go to war. This is how I used fasting at that time:

> In addition to my praying, I fasted. God alone could keep my husband from going to war. There was nothing I could do, and there was nothing Jim could do. There was no human way out. So, I began to fast on December 4. I decided to break my fast each day at sundown, a format which followed the Jewish model and which happened to correspond to the 5 P.M. close of all Army offices....On that first day, I also decided that

> I would fast until I knew Jim was not going
> to the Persian Gulf or, if he did go, until he
> came back—or died. That was my covenant
> with God.[3]

Are there any issues you are struggling with that only God
can resolve? Why not cast your burdens and cares and anx-
ieties on the Lord (1 Peter 5:7)? A time of prayer and fasting
might be needed.

Following Our Calling to Godliness

What are some things you can do this week to follow in
Anna's footsteps? Add your personal specifics for each, along
with your own *whys* and *whats* and *hows*.

✓ *Pray*—the more we pray, the more we're aware of the
   presence of the Lord.

✓ *Purpose*—to be more aware of God's presence.

✓ *Praise the Lord*—it's a good thing!

✓ *Praise Him some more*—develop a "praising heart."

✓ *Pick a point for meditation*—and tune your heart to the Lord.

✓ *Prize*—your high calling to reverent behavior.

✓ *Plan*—to act in ways that attract attention to the Lord rather than to yourself.

✓ *Ponder*—your behavior and your choices. What are they "telling" about you?

Looking Upward

Please read the "Looking Upward" section in your book again. As you consider the contents of this chapter and God's high calling to you, write out your personal "Prayer for Godly Living."

Chapter Two

Essential 1

Godliness—An Essential for Godly Living

*"the older women [are to] be
reverent in behavior"*
—TITUS 2:3

 Begin this lesson by reading chapter 2, "God-liness—An Essential for Godly Living," in your personal copy of *A Woman's High Calling*. Note here any new truths or challenges that stand out to you.

As I said in our book, this section is all about making the essentials of God's calling prominent features of our lives. As we begin this chapter, think back to chapter 1, and then write out why you think "godliness" or reverent behavior was placed first on God's list of essentials for godly living in Titus 2:3-5.

Meet Mary Jane

Can you think of a "Mary Jane"—an example of godliness—from your own life? Describe how she models godliness for you.

If you can't think of an example at this time, ask God to bring a woman who exemplifies godliness into your life. Pray that, before you finish reading your book and working through this *Growth and Study Guide*, God will provide a model of godliness you can follow!

The Meditations of the Mind

Two key areas of our life where godliness must be nurtured are the mind and the mouth. King David had a similar perspective. Write out his words in Psalm 19:14 and make them yours:

Make a decision each day to dwell on the Lord. Good choices have long-term results. A daily decision to dwell on the Lord will bring greater godliness to your life. What will you do today to dwell on the Lord that will "set the sail" toward greater godliness?

For help with this exercise, notice the willful focus of these writers. What decisions did each one make?

Joshua 1:8—

Psalm 5:3—

Psalm 16:8—

Make sure your thoughts meet the guidelines of Philippians 4:8. List those guidelines here and give a brief definition of each from your dictionary.

—

—

—

—

—

—

—

—

How do you think meditating on these godly "things" will contribute to a life of godliness?

Master the great hymns of the faith. Singing the old time-honored hymns of the faith seems to be a thing of the past. But put your hands on some hymnbooks, select several hymns that speak to your heart, and memorize their lyrics. Then make a joyful noise unto the Lord (Psalm 100:1)! What hymn would you like to begin with?

Memorize Scripture. The mind is like any other muscle in your body. If it is exercised, it will become stronger. A wonderful (and uplifting!) way to strengthen your mind is to memorize Scripture. You may want to choose several verses from the above questions to memorize. Or choose several of your own. List them here. Then write each one out on a 3x5 card and make it a goal to memorize them this week. (Check here when this is done_____.)

Verse #1—

Verse #2—

Mark out certain times each day for praising God. Have you picked out a time (or times!) each day when you want to give praise to God? Note below where...when...and what you will do.

> There is a great market for religious experience in our world; there is little enthusiasm for the patient acquisition of virtue, little inclination to sign up for a long apprenticeship in what earlier generations of Christians called holiness.[4]

Guidelines for the Mouth

The Bible gives many positive results of godly speech. What positive results do these verses offer?

Proverbs 15:1a—

Proverbs 16:24—

Proverbs 21:23—

I can't help but have you look up Proverbs 31:26 in your Bible. This is my prayer for myself, and I'm sure you desire such godly speech for yourself as well! Write out this godly woman's guidelines for *her* mouth...and then let's look at three other women whose speech set them apart as women possessing the high calling of God on their lives.

Anna—Read Luke 2:38 again and note how Anna used her mouth.

Elizabeth—Now read Luke 1:39-45. These are the only recorded words of Elizabeth. What do her words indicate about her reverence for God?

Mary—Continue reading in Luke 1:46-55. The majority of Mary's spoken words are recorded here. Her mouth spoke forth *from* (and spoke *of!*) a heart filled with Scripture. Compare the similarities of her "Magnificat" with Hannah's song in 1 Samuel 2:1-10:

Mary (Luke 1:46-55)   *Hannah* (1 Samuel 2:1-10)

These women set wonderful examples for us, don't they? And here are two more guidelines for the mouth to move us toward more godly speech.

Speak of the Lord. What steps will you take in your everyday life to "speak of the Lord" more often?

Speak well of others. What steps will you take to "speak well of others"?

To Sum It Up...

In the book I asked the hard question, "What usually comes out of your mouth?" Answer that question now.

How do the speech patterns of the godly women we've looked at in this lesson and the two thoughts above assist you in establishing godly guidelines for your speech?

> A holy life has a voice. It speaks when the tongue is silent, and is either a constant attraction or a perpetual reproof.[5]

Looking Upward

Please read the "Looking Upward" section in your book again. As you consider the contents of this chapter and God's high calling to you, write out your personal "Prayer for Godly Living."

Chapter Three

Essential 2

A Woman's High Calling to Godly Speech

"the older women [are to] be...
not slanderers"
—TITUS 2:3

Begin this lesson by reading chapter 3, "A Woman's High Calling to Godly Speech," in your personal copy of *A Woman's High Calling.* Note here any new truths or challenges that stand out to you.

God's Calling to Godly Speech

Glance back through your notes on "Learning About Godliness" from chapter 1. Now put in your own words why godliness and gossip cannot coexist.

Learning About Gossip

We learned that the word "slander" comes from the Greek word *diabolos,* meaning a malicious gossip, a slanderer, or a false accuser. Look up these verses that use the same Greek word *diabolos.* Then write out the context of its use.

Matthew 4:1—

John 6:70—

1 Timothy 3:11—

2 Timothy 3:2-3—

Titus 2:3—

What lessons from these scriptures become obvious as we seek to become godly women?

Aspiring to Godly Speech

What a wonderful high calling—to aspire to godly speech! I can think of several reasons why you and I should aspire to godly speech:

- Godly speech is a mark of maturity.
- Godly speech is a mandate for godly ministry.
- Godly speech is a high calling from God.

Kind words are short to speak,
but their echoes are endless.

Kind words do not wear out the tongue—
so speak them.

Now add several of your own reasons to this list that should cause us to aspire to godly speech:

§

§

§

Life-Lessons Learned from Others

Read about the instances of slanderous speech in these women from your Bible. And don't forget to record the results of their malicious attacks!

Potiphar's wife (Genesis 39:1-20)—

Jezebel (1 Kings 21:1-14)—

Martha (Luke 10:38-42)—

The Facts About Gossip

Do you know "the facts about gossip"? The facts the Bible reveals to us? Let's learn them now.

The Source of Gossip—Who did we learn is the source of malicious gossip and slander?

*The Causes of Gossip—*Take these sinful "causes" to heart:

§ *An evil heart—*What does Luke 6:45 name as a cause of evil speech?

   And what does Matthew 15:18-19 name as a cause of evil speech and deeds?

§ *Hatred—*Poor David! To whom (or what) did he attribute his demise in Psalm 109:3?

§ *Foolishness—*Proverbs 10:18 is very direct! What is its message to your heart?

§ *Idleness—*Before this book is over, you'll be well familiar with 1 Timothy 5:13! What does it say about idleness? And how did idleness affect the young women spoken of in this verse?

Now that you've identified a few of the root causes of gossip, "dig around" in your own heart. Confess and admit to the sin of gossip—each and every time you do it. Then pinpoint the cause—was it the overflow of an evil heart? Are you harboring hatred toward another? Do you need to ask

God for wisdom so that you don't open your mouth in foolishness? Is idleness a problem? Be honest.

The Public Consequences of Gossip—Gossip always leads to disastrous public consequences. Can you think of instances you know of that illustrate the following consequences of gossip? Briefly describe the situation...but be careful not to name names. That would be gossiping!

Gossip separates friends—

Gossip causes strife—

Gossip causes discord in the body of Christ—

Gossip is the same as murder—

How should the memory of these events—and their awful consequences—affect you the next time you are tempted to gossip?

The Personal Consequences of Gossip—Let's move from "others" to yourself! How are these "givens" true?

Gossip jeopardizes our ministry—

Gossip harms us—

Gossip can never be taken back—

> The difference between a smart man and a wise man is that a smart man knows what to say and a wise man knows whether to say it or not.[6]

What conclusions can you draw...and what further commitments will you make to put away "all bitterness, wrath, anger, clamor, and evil speaking...[and] all malice" out of your mouth? (See Ephesians 4:31 and Colossians 3:8.)

As I stated in this section of our book, I'm endeavoring to make *godly speech* a lifetime goal. I want to follow in the footsteps of my Lord, whose lips spoke no sin. Whose lips spoke words of love and kindness. Whose words ministered to the outcasts and the downhearted. Is this your goal as well? (I pray that it is!) You'll be asked in the "Looking Upward" section to write out your personal prayer. And as you put it in writing, dear one, reflect on David's resolve:

> I said, "I will guard my ways,
> Lest I sin with my tongue;
> I will restrain my mouth with a muzzle."
> —PSALM 39:1

Looking Upward

Please read the "Looking Upward" section in your book again. As you consider the contents of this chapter and God's high calling to you, write out your personal "Prayer for Godly Living."

Chapter Four

Essential

Godly Speech—An Essential for Godly Living

"the older women [are to] be
...not slanderers"
—Titus 2:3

Begin this lesson by reading chapter 4, "Godly Speech—An Essential for Godly Living," in your personal copy of *A Woman's High Calling*. Note here any new truths or challenges that stand out to you.

Meet Some of My Sisters

I so enjoyed sharing with you about some of my older women and sisters-in-Christ who exemplify godliness and godly speech to me. Truly (as we've noted throughout our study) one picture is worth a thousand words! Now list and describe some of the women who minister to you and model godly living to you through their life and speech. When you're done, consider writing each one of them a note of thanks and encouragement. Godly living always comes with a high price tag!

A Moment of Review

I don't believe a review of gossip and our speech would be complete without a look at a passage of Scripture that directly addresses our problem of speech and the use (or *mis*use!) of our tongue, James 3:5-12. After your initial read-through, look specifically at verses 5 through 8. Then write out several of the graphic descriptions of the tongue James used:

Next, read verses 9 through 12 again and write out several inconsistencies of the tongue (and don't forget to marvel along with James at these incredible inconsistencies!):

In my Bible study on James, *Growing in Wisdom & Faith,*[7] I quoted Dr. Gene Getz's comments about our speech, which are based on the passage from James 3:

Three Categories of Gossip

The first kind of gossip is malicious gossip.... Malicious gossip is consciously and deliberately hurtful. It is based in envy and rooted in flagrant selfishness. It is designed to break up relationships and destroy friendships. And it can manifest itself in all kinds of evil deeds.

The second kind of gossip is rationalization. It is far more subtle than malicious gossip. What makes rationalization so dangerous is that it often results from self-deception. Rooted and based in the same motives as malicious gossip, the person who rationalizes has convinced herself (himself) that she is doing it for "the good" of the other person. She may disguise it as "prayer interest" and "personal concern." Nevertheless rationalization is very destructive.

The third kind of gossip is "innocent" gossip. This involves a person who truly is concerned, but who is, to a certain extent, unwise and insensitive to other people's feelings. Innocent gossip is sometimes motivated by a desire to be "helpful," but in reality, the gossiper may be trying to prove to others "how helpful she really is." In this situation there is a very fine line between "selfish" and "unselfish" motives. All Christians must beware of this kind of gossip.

How can you use these three measuring sticks the next time you are tempted to gossip about others?

And speaking of gossiping about others, who do you tend to talk about and why?

Finally, in which category of gossip given by Dr. Getz do you tend to fall? What will you do to correct your ways?

Moving Forward

I mentioned in this section of your book that Proverbs 31:26 teaches us two guidelines for our speech—wisdom and kindness. Write out the following verses about both wisdom and kindness and select and star several to commit to memory. Note the central teaching in each scripture about speech. Then make both of these biblical mandates for godly speech a lifelong study and goal.

Wisdom and Kindness—First, write out Proverbs 31:26 here.

Wisdom—

Job 28:28—

Proverbs 15:33—

Psalms 90:12—

James 1:5—

James 3:17—

Kindness—

Galatians 5:22—

Colossians 3:12—

2 Peter 1:7—

We'll study kindness later in our book, but for now note God's calling to speech that is both kind *and* wise...and then let's consider ways to make progress in this practice that is vital to godliness.

Making Progress

Did you learn something about the practicalities of making progress against gossip from the four key questions given in your book? I gave you a list of my own personal "how-to's"— but now, as I ask those questions of you again, what will be *your* strategy for dealing with gossip? Make your own list of "how-to's," or pick several of mine. But whatever you do, under each question write out two or three things you will do.

Question #1—"How can I avoid gossiping?"

Question #2—"How can I work at eliminating gossip from my life?" And don't forget the "four *Ts*":

T ime—

T elephone—

T alk—

T arry—

Question #3—"How can I make permanent changes in the way that I talk?"

Question #4—"What should I do when others gossip?"

It would be oh-so-easy to get discouraged about our mouth and what comes out of it, wouldn't it? But take heart as you read these encouraging words, again from Dr. Gene Getz!

> If no human being can control the tongue, why bother trying? Because even if we do not achieve perfect control of it in this life, we can still learn enough control to reduce the damage it can do. It is better to fight a fire than to go around setting new ones! Remember that we are not fighting the tongue's fire on our own strength. The Holy Spirit will give us increasing powers to monitor and control what we say. As Christians we are not perfect, but we should never stop growing....God works to change us from the inside out. As the Holy Spirit purifies our hearts, he also gives us self-control so that we will speak words that please God.[8]

Also I've adapted John Wesley's covenant slightly. Once again, as you write out your prayer in the "Looking Upward" section, perhaps these words will fuel your heart response!

I will not listen to gossip. If I hear it,
I will not believe gossip.
I will quickly go to the one whose name was
*   mentioned in the gossip.*
I will speak to no one until I speak to the one
*   mentioned in the gossip. Then,*
I will mention to no one thereafter that gossip.

Looking Upward

Please read the "Looking Upward" section in your book again. As you consider the contents of this chapter and God's high calling to you, write out your personal "Prayer for Godly Living."

Chapter Five

Essential 3

A Woman's High Calling to Personal Discipline

"the older women [are to] be...
not given to much wine"
*—*TITUS 2:3

Begin this lesson by reading chapter 5, "A Woman's High Calling to Personal Discipline," in your personal copy of *A Woman's High Calling*. Note here any new truths or challenges that stand out to you.

Read again the thoughts on discipline by J.O. Sanders. Write down the words or phrases (or challenges) that impressed you the most. Why did you choose them?

Considering God's Calling to Personal Discipline

Titus 2:3—Write out God's high calling to personal discipline and discuss why Paul may have put "not slanderers, not given to much wine" together as he gave guidance regarding the older women.

1 Timothy 3:11—These words were written to the wives of the leaders of the church and/or the women leaders in the church at Ephesus. In either case, women then were to, and we women today as well...were to exhibit certain qualities. Compare Paul's *positive* calling in 1 Timothy 3:11 with his admonition in the *negative* to the women in the churches on Crete (Titus 2:3).

- ẟ First the *negative*—"The older women likewise, that they be reverent in behavior, not slanderers, *not given to much wine,* teachers of good things" (Titus 2:3, emphasis added).

- ẟ Next the *positive*—"Likewise their wives must be reverent, not slanderers, *temperate,* faithful in all things" (1 Timothy 3:11, emphasis added).

Just a note: One observation from these two references reveals two letters, two churches, two locations...and one problem—gossip! Gossip was a problem almost 2000 years ago. Do you think it's a problem in your church today? Please explain your answer and then read this sad tale.

On Sunday a restaurant manager designates two rooms as a non-smoking area to accommodate churchgoers who come in for a bite to eat after their evening service. A busboy there said he was glad to see the large number of non-smokers. But then he added, "They may not smoke, but you ought to hear them gossip. If we had a non-gossip section, nobody would be there."[9]

Considering the Problem

Do you agree or disagree with the apostles' belief that "Christianity *must* and *could* deliver all believers from bondage to wine" (or any other "problem")? Please explain your answer.

Wine may have been needed as a liquid drink in Bible times, but the Bible also contains strong words of caution about its use. Look up the following verses and jot down these cautions:

Ephesians 5:18—

Proverbs 20:1—

Proverbs 23:30—talks about lingering long at wine and searching for mixed wine. What are some of the results of such lingering and searching (verse 29)?

Isaiah 5:11—

Now that you have a little understanding of the problems of wine both in biblical times and in our society today, write out a few sentences of your own that discuss the role of sobriety and temperance in a woman who is to be "reverent in behavior" (Titus 2:3).

Considering the Meaning

Who is called to personal discipline and temperance? Look up these verses that speak of discipline and temperance.

1 Timothy 3:2—

1 Timothy 3:11—

Titus 2:2—

What does the Bible say about temperance and discipline?

1 Thessalonians 5:6—

1 Thessalonians 5:8—

2 Timothy 4:5—

1 Peter 1:13—

1 Peter 4:7—

1 Peter 5:8—

Now underline the repeated words from these verses. What words seem to be repeated the most?

What does temperance and self-control mean? Look up temperance and self-control in your own English dictionary. Record some of the definitions you find there.

Temperance—

Self-control—

Looking into the Mirror

Write out your answers to the questions found in this section. Are there any areas that are excessive or "out of control"...

...regarding your use of food and drink?

...regarding your speech patterns?

...regarding your emotions?

How would you describe yourself? Circle one and then explain your choice.

excited	agitated	bothered
reasonable	rational	level-headed

How About an Exercise?

I hope you enjoyed what some of my friends wrote as their definitions of this powerful essential of godliness. And, as I said in your book, I want you to take what you're learning from this chapter and do the exercise for yourself—write your own definition of temperance and moderation here.

Considering Two Questions

Question #1—Why is this godly quality of personal discipline an essential for us?

Why do you think we need to possess discipline in order to qualify as a teacher of good things to the younger women?

Question #2—Why should we desire to answer this high calling from God?

And which "imagine..." from the book (pages 76–78) do you most desire, and why?

Daily Dogged Discipline

I'm a great believer in what I have sometimes called "the daily dogged discipline" of the Christian life. The greatest enemies of discipline are laziness and emotionalism. Lazy people can't be bothered to acquire disciplined habits, and emotional or temperamental people prefer to live by their feelings. The "I'll see what I feel like" attitude is certain to end in disaster. We do not read God's Word and pray only on the days when we feel like it, but every day (better twice a day), whether we feel like it or not. We do not join the Lord's people for worship on those Sundays when we feel like it, but every Sunday, whether we feel like it or not, because it is the Lord's Day. Do we only come to work when we feel like it? Then why should we give our heavenly Lord a service inferior to what we give our earthly employer? We "serve the Lord Christ" (Colossians 3:24). Then let's give Him better service, greater faithfulness, and more discipline than to any human master.[10]

—John Stott

Looking Upward

Please read the "Looking Upward" section in your book again. As you consider the contents of this chapter and God's high calling to you, write out your personal "Prayer for Godly Living."

Chapter Six

Essential

Personal Discipline— An Essential for Godly Living

"the older women [are to] be...
not give to much wine"
—TITUS 2:3

Begin this lesson by reading chapter 6, "Personal Discipline—An Essential for Godly Living," in your personal copy of *A Woman's High Calling*. Note here any new truths or challenges that stand out to you.

Your Physical Life

As we begin this chapter on personal discipline, I want you to evaluate your *physical life* for areas of excess. I st the areas where you need to develop a greater depth or elf-control. Be very honest with yourself.

Now that you've listed some areas that need greater discipline, use the following "lifestyle" practices to develop a strategy for strengthening the areas you chose. Be sure to look up each Scripture reference and note its teaching on this vital area of discipline.

1. *Think of models*—First, think of those you know who model God's brand of personal discipline. Briefly describe what they *do*...and don't *do*...that you admire, how they act under pressure. Why did you choose them?

   Then look in your Bible at these men and women of strength. Again, note what they did and didn't do.

   § *The Proverbs 31 woman*—Proverbs 31:17,25. What is her message to you?

   § *The apostle Paul*—1 Corinthians 9:24-27. What is his message to you?

   § *The apostle Paul's advice to Timothy*—1 Timothy 4:8 and 2 Timothy 2:3-6. What is the message to you?

   § *The writer of Hebrews' advice*—Hebrews 12:1-2. What is his message to you?

2. *Read on self-control and life management*—There is a sea of books and articles on physical discipline you can select! And as you can tell, the men and women of the Bible provide excellent reading material, too!

3. *Look to God's Spirit*—Galatians 5:22-23.

4. *"Make no provision for the flesh"*—Romans 13:14.

5. *Just say NO!*—2 Timothy 2:22.

6. *Pray*—Write out a specific prayer to God for each area where you need His help to overcome your area of indulgence. (Perhaps you can incorporate this exercise in your "Personal Prayer" at the end of this lesson.)

Your Emotional Life

When it comes to greater emotional strength and stability, we can all use a little help! Again, evaluate your *emotional life* for weak areas and write them down here. Then use these practical steps to help you develop a strategy for bettering your emotional soundness. Don't fail to look up every scripture. God's Word is one of our greatest resources!

1. *Think of models*—Note their names here and sketch out what it is in them that speaks of a strength in the inner man.

   ℘ In addition to those you think of, there is always the Proverbs 31 woman. Scan God's brief sketch of her life full of little daily disciplines (Proverbs 31:10-31) and see how they send a monumental message to you and me. Jot down the instances or hints of her emotional strength.

   ℘ Next look at an incident in the life of Esther. Esther's husband, the king, had just issued an edict that allowed all Jews to be murdered— including her! Read Esther 4:10-16 and make note of her "battle plan," remembering that wisdom always has a plan (Proverbs 21:5)! Rather than fall apart, this woman of steel went to battle.

2. *Cultivate regular quiet times*—Psalm 46:10.

3. *Count on God*—Psalm 46:1-2. How is He described here?

> There is a restlessness and a fretfulness in these days, which stand like two granite walls against godliness. Contentment is almost necessary to godliness and godliness is absolutely necessary to contentment. A very restless man will never be a very godly man, and a very godly man will never be a very restless man.[11]

4. *Work the study guide*—Congratulations, you are doing just that! I'm sure you can already see some differences this study is making in your life. Keep moving forward!

Your Practical Life

As I said, the practical exercise of planning is an essential part of the process of developing a disciplined life. I'm sure you've heard many sayings like these!

> "Aim at nothing and you will hit it every time."
>
> ↩
>
> "Plan ahead to stay ahead."
>
> ↩
>
> "Plan your day or someone else will plan it for you."
>
> ↩
>
> "God has a wonderful plan for your life...
> and so does everyone else!"

1. *Use your mind to plan for victory!* What message does Proverbs 21:5 have for us in this practical discipline of planning?

   What steps can you take to make planning a regular part of your daily activities?

2. *Use your mind to pinpoint the "tightrope times" each day*...the times when things could—or do!—fall apart. There could be more than one time.

   § Tightrope time #1—

      What is your plan for dealing with this time each day?

   § Tightrope time #2—

      What is your plan for dealing with this time each day?

(For a bonus blessing, read about the "tightrope time" the godly and disciplined Abigail faced in 1 Samuel 25:2-42. Make a list of the wise ways she handled her life-threatening situation!)

As I said in your book, God will show you the best way to live for Him. After reading this chapter and going through these exercises, what one thing can you bring to God in prayer and ask for His help in so that you can (with His more-than-able help) live a more disciplined life in that area? Answer this question...and then let's look upward.

Looking Upward

Please read the "Looking Upward" section in your book again. As you consider the contents of this chapter and God's high calling to you, write out your personal "Prayer for Godly Living."

Chapter Seven

A Woman's High Calling to Encourage Others

"the older women [are to] be...
teachers of good things"
—TITUS 2:3

 Begin this lesson by reading chapter 7, "A Woman's High Calling to Encourage Others," in your personal copy of *A Woman's High Calling*. Note here any new truths or challenges that stand out to you.

After reading the introduction to this chapter, how would you answer these questions:

"Where are the older women?"

"What are the older women doing to train up a new generation in your church?"

"Is there any curriculum in your church to develop both the older and younger women?"

A Definition

Break down the Greek word *kalodidaskalos* and its meaning as presented in your book:

kalos—

didaskalos—

For the purpose of understanding, how did your book define this essential for godly living?

Are you a younger woman? (Your answer should be yes!) Then write down the names of several godly older women (in age or in maturity) who might teach, disciple, mentor, and encourage you to "be of sound mind and to have self-control."

A Few Words of Explanation

There are two God-given platforms for us as women from which we can teach and encourage others. What are you doing in...

The Church? Who are those in your church that you could teach and encourage? Are you doing so...or at least preparing to do so? Describe your ministry...or your preparations.

The Home? Who are those in this "home" category that you have the most opportunity to teach? Daughters? Daughters-in-law? Granddaughters? Nieces? Name each one here...and don't forget to make a special prayer list or page and start praying for each one each day! (Check here when this is done____.)

The Content—God sets down the curriculum for us to teach—and learn!—in Titus 2:3-5. What areas of this curriculum do you need to grow in, and how are you going to do it?

❧   Loving your husband—

❧   Loving your children—

❧   Being sensible—

❧   Being pure—

❧   Being a homemaker—

❧   Being good and kind—

❧   Following your husband's leadership—

In what areas have you developed to the point that you can now pass on your information and experience to another woman? (And just a practical hint—since these qualities and those mentioned in Titus 2:3—godliness, godly speech, personal discipline, and encouraging others—make up the curriculum, why not set up ten file folders, one each for the ten essentials for godly living, and begin filing information there to pass on to someone else? Check here when this is done_____.)

The Purpose—Everyone needs encouragement. How does the biblical definition of "encouragement" differ from your traditional understanding?

And what is the purpose of such encouragement, or what is to be the end-product?

Is there someone who needs your encouragement today?

The Technique—List the two techniques we are to employ when we "teach" others:

—

—

> One of the highest of human duties is the duty of encouragement....It is easy to laugh at men's ideals; it is easy to pour cold water on their enthusiasm; it is easy to discourage others. The world is full of discouragers. We have a Christian duty to encourage one another. Many a time a word of praise or thanks or appreciation or cheer has kept a man on his feet. Blessed is the man who speaks such a word.[12]

A Few Examples from the Bible

How do these godly examples model the teaching and encouraging of younger women for us?

Elizabeth with Mary (Luke 1:1-56)—Describe this electric meeting between older and younger woman. What was the "content" of their meeting together? Of their sharing?

The true widows (1 Timothy 5:2-10)—I know this may seem like a repeat, but remember—repetition is the mother of all skill! So...jot down what "good things" these older women had to pass on to the younger women:

The Woman of Proverbs 31 (Proverbs 31:10-31)—Scan these enlightening verses. Note three or four "topics" you wish this woman could sit down and teach you!

Now, pray for opportunities to be—and to be with—such women!

Opposites

What negatives do these women model for us?

The young widows (1 Timothy 5:13)—

Euodia and Syntyche (Philippians 4:1-2)—

Miriam (Numbers 12:1-15)—

A Few Questions

1. *Are you a younger woman?* Have you yet sought out an older woman to teach and encourage you in this God-given curriculum of essentials for godly living? Are you praying about being discipled or mentored? About setting up a time to talk with a more mature woman? About the areas where you need help? Growing and learning is God's assignment for you—along with preparing to teach these "good things" to others in the future!

2. *Are you an older woman?* Write down the names of several younger women (in age or in maturity) to whom you might impart some of the "good things" God has taught you over the years. If none come to mind, pray for observing eyes and that God would bring someone into your life to teach. (If you have daughters, start there, remembering they are not in an optional category—they *are* God's assignment to you! You *are* to teach them!)

A Final Challenge

Have you yet accepted your role to become a "teacher of good things"? Why or why not?

What are you doing to prepare to teach others?

How available are you to the women of your church?

How aware are you of the younger women around you?

Have you been praying about your teaching assignment from God?

Looking Upward

Please read the "Looking Upward" section in your book again. As you consider the contents of this chapter and God's high calling to you, write out your personal "Prayer for Godly Living."

Chapter Eight

Essential

Encouraging Others—
An Essential for Godly Living

"the older women [are to] be...
teachers of good things"
—Titus 2:3

Begin this lesson by reading chapter 8, "Encouraging Others—An Essential for Godly Living," in your personal copy of *A Woman's High Calling*. Note here any new truths or challenges that stand out to you.

As we step into this lesson, remember our two God-given assignments. What are they?

First, we are to be...

Second, we are to be...

What We Must Be

Which of the thoughts or quotations about teaching spoke the loudest to your heart? And why? (And remember, as a general rule, teachers teach more by what they *are* than by what they *say!*)

Write out, once again, your understanding of what each of these essentials for godly living means. Then assess where you think you are in each of these ten essential areas in your own journey toward maturity. As we finish looking at the essentials for godliness given in the third verse of Titus 2, scan back through the preceding chapters and lessons and give yourself one more assignment for growth in these prerequisites for any woman seeking to answer God's high callings upon her life.

    § "Dignified" means—

        Lord, help me to grow in this essential by...

    § "Not malicious gossips" means—

        Lord, help me to grow in this essential by...

    § "Temperate and self-controlled" means—

        Lord, help me to grow in this essential by...

§ "Teachers of good things" means—

Lord, help me to grow in this essential by...

What We Must Do

In your book I asked a number of questions to help us make sure we are growing. And I'm repeating them here for your honest evaluation. As always, write out what you can do to grow this week—even a step you can take today.

Do you need to be discipled?

Do you need to look for a mentor?

Do you need to spend some quality time with an older woman?

Are you on the path to learning about these ten good things, these ten essentials for godly living?

Are there gaps in your conduct, life, skills, and disciplines that need to be filled?

Are there things you need to learn?

Books you need to read?

Classes you need to attend?

Who We Must Teach

If you have children, what are you doing to teach them?

Your daughter(s)—

Your son(s)—

Look at these scriptures and write out in your own words why it's important to teach your own daughters and sons about godliness:

1 Timothy 2:9-15—

1 Timothy 3:4 and 12—

Proverbs 31:1-2—

The young women—what are you doing to teach them?

Is there a particular age group of younger women that you might teach?

What We Must Teach

Hopefully by now, we understand that Titus 2:3-5 *is* what we must teach!

Reread Luke 1:39-56 and jot down what happened at this meeting between an older and younger woman. If you are currently meeting with any younger women, are you paying attention to—

spiritual instruction? What do you think two women who have a bond in Jesus Christ, who are set apart from the world, who are indwelt by the Holy Spirit, and who love the Word of God, *should* be talking about when they get together?

practical instruction? What kind of assignments do you think a woman who is supposed to be a teacher of good things *should* give to her "pupil"? Study questions? Checklists? Recommended reading lists? Homework? Worksheets? Accountability forms? Prayer assignments?

Evaluate your own discipleship philosophy and methods. Does what you are currently doing meet God's high standards? Are you working at passing on God's good things to those you are encouraging? Please explain...and perhaps write out what you will do to "beef up" your get-togethers.

Optional assignment—If you are serious about growing into a teacher—or a better teacher!—of these good things from God, purchase and read *The Master Plan of Evangelism* by Robert E. Coleman (Grand Rapids, MI: Baker Book House, 1993). Jesus discipled by following these eight principles:[13]

selection	demonstration
association	delegation
consecration	supervision
impartation	reproduction

Looking Upward

Please read the "Looking Upward" section in your book again. As you consider the contents of this chapter and God's high calling to you, write out your personal "Prayer for Godly Living."

Chapter Nine

ssential

A Woman's High Calling
to Her Marriage

*"...admonish the young women to
love their husbands..."*
—TITUS 2:4

Begin this lesson by reading chapter 9, "A Woman's High Calling to Her Marriage," in your personal copy of *A Woman's High Calling*. Note here any new truths or challenges that stand out to you.

Before we consider the specifics of marriage, look at the following passages in the Bible to familiarize yourself with what God says are the roles and responsibilities of a Christian wife. Read quickly and jot down the key thoughts from each scripture.

Genesis 2:18-25—

Genesis 3 (pay particular attention to verses 1-6 and 14-19)—

1 Corinthians 11:3-12—

2 Corinthians 11:3—

1 Timothy 2:9-15—

The Role of a Wife

A wife is to help her husband—write out Genesis 2:18.

I'm sure you've heard of (and maybe even keep!) a "Honey, Do..." list of things your dear husband can (and maybe needs) to do around the house. But have you ever thought of yourself as your husband's helper? Make a list of a few things you, "Honey," can "do" to help *him* with—

§   His responsibilities—

§   His tasks—

§   His roles—

§   His work—

§   His callings from God—

Now go back through this list and circle one thing you will do today to help your husband in each area. Then get out your calendar and note on it one thing you will do each day this week to help your husband. (Check here when this is done____, and then chuckle over this thought!)

~

If you do housework at $200 a week,
that's domestic service.
If you do it for nothing, that's matrimony.

~

A wife is to follow her husband—write out Genesis 3:16—

§ And Ephesians 5:22 and 24—

§ And Colossians 3:18—

§ And 1 Peter 3:1—

Before you panic, let me quickly tell you that I began this process of following and submitting to my Jim in a very tiny area—as tiny as a donut! Jim wanted our family to stop by the donut shop on the way to church each Sunday. And I, of course, had a long list of reasons why I thought it wasn't a good idea. Well, you guessed it—one Sunday I "submitted." I said nothing. We went to the donut shop...and had a wonderful Lord's Day...and made going to the donut shop a standing Sunday morning family tradition!

Now, can you pinpoint one such tiny area in your marriage where you can begin to honor your husband (and the Lord) by following him? What will you do about this area of obedience this week?

And while you're at it, make a list of larger areas where you are failing to follow your husband. Begin praying...and doing what it takes for you to answer God's high calling to you to follow your husband's leadership.

A wife is to respect her husband—write out Ephesians 5:33.

Now write out the definition of respect given in your book: "To respect a husband means...

What will you do today, right in your own home, to demonstrate your respect toward your husband? Pray to make such acts the habit of your life!

A wife is to love her husband—read Titus 2:3-5 in your Bible. Be sure to note the high calling from God to you as a wife found in verse 4.

The Love of a Wife

A definition—Jot down what you learned about the definition of "loving" your husband.

A decision—Have you made your decision "to love your husband" as Titus 2:4 describes it? How can you set about to develop a deeper friendship with your husband?

An evaluation—Evaluate the "love quotient" in your marriage. How will you "invest" the "treasure" of more time and effort and care into loving your husband?

~

*A successful marriage requires
falling in love many times,
always with the same person.*[14]

~

The Tales of Two Wives

First the positive, the Shulamite—Look at Song of Solomon 5:9. Could you say the same about your husband? Why or why not?

Next the negative, Michal—What is your mouth and heart filled with toward your "beloved"? Give a specific instance.

A Word of Encouragement

Note here how and when you will *pray* for your husband, how and when you will *praise* your husband, and how and when you will *pamper* your husband. And, of course, you will want to make these acts—praying, praising, and pampering—the habit of your life!

§ Pray—

§ Praise—

§ Pamper—

A Word of Warning

As you think about what the *world* tells wives versus what the *Word of God* tells them, what dangerous differences do you detect?

Looking Upward

Please read the "Looking Upward" section in your book again. As you consider the contents of this chapter and God's high calling to you, write out your personal "Prayer for Godly Living."

Chapter Ten

Loving Your Husband—
An Essential for Godly Living

"...admonish the young women to
love their husbands..."
—TITUS 2:4

 Begin this lesson by reading chapter 10, "Loving Your Husband—An Essential for Godly Living," in your personal copy of *A Woman's High Calling*. Note here any new truths or challenges that stand out to you.

Becoming Best Friends

Begin by making a list of the many "little things" you do for a best girl friend.

Is your husband receiving the same attention from you? Or better yet, is your husband receiving *more* attention from you than a mere girl friend receives? Please explain, and then write out how you plan to place your friendship with your husband above that of a friendship with any other person.

Saying "I Love You"

In your book I listed a dozen or so ways to say "I love you" to your precious husband. After answering these questions, see if you can add to the list.

1. *Make the choice to love your husband.*
   How does the final phrase of Titus 2:5 motivate you and move you to make this choice?

2. *Make the choice to love your husband before or ahead of your children.*
   Do you have children? If so, does your husband hold "first place" or do the children? Please explain, and then write out some better ways to ensure that your husband is Number One in your heart and home.

3. *Submit yourself to be "taught" to love your husband.*
   Do you have an "older woman" who is assisting you in learning how to better love your husband?

   How active are you in teaching others to do the same?

~

*Matrimony is the only state
that allows a woman to work
eighteen hours a day.*

~

4. *Set up a prayer book or prayer page for your husband.*
   "The greatest gift you can give your husband is the gift of
   lifting his name and his needs before the throne of God."
   Stop right this minute and set up at least a prayer page
   for your precious husband. Better yet, do you have a
   blank book—you know, one of the little wordless books?
   Find a beautiful one that helps you to do the beautiful
   work of praying for your man. (Check here when this is
   done_____.)

5. *Write a letter to God.*
   When I first began to grapple with God's high calling to
   me to "love" my husband, I wrote out my commitment to
   answer God's high calling in a letter and prayer to God.
   In fact, I still have the letter these 25-plus years later! Why
   don't you make your commitment a matter of record and
   write your own letter to God? (Check here when this is
   done_____.)

6. *Cultivate willful love.*
   How is your "will" power? Write out at least three "I
   will's" here that will help you to follow through (by God's
   grace!) on "the duty of love."

   § I will...

   § I will...

   § I will...

7. *Listen to God's Word, not the world.*

Is the pattern of your daily life one of listening to gossip...or to God's Word? To trivia...or to truth? To worldly wisdom...or to God's wisdom? To talk shows...or to teaching tapes? To friends on the phone...or to answers from the Bible about life's issues? (I'm sure you're getting the point!) The bottom-line question is, are you willfully and consciously increasing the time you spend in God's Word and decreasing the time you spend listening to the philosophy of this world (Colossians 2:8)? As always, please explain...and then make a schedule for tomorrow (and for the rest of your life!) that ensures that you listen to God's Word, not to the world. This, dear one, is one way we answer any and all of God's high callings to us to be godly women!

8. *Read daily on marriage.*

Whether you are a "reader" or not, you can learn to become a better wife by reading. Talk with your Christian friends to find out about—or make your own list of—three books on marriage.

Book #1—

Book #2—

Book #3—

Now make your own grid or checksheet (or list on your calendar) that will reflect the "little" act of reading just five minutes a day on marriage. (Check here when this is done_____.)

9. *Do the works of love heartily.*
   Write out Colossians 3:23 here.

   How do you think the "heart" of this scripture can make a difference in your out-"working" of God's role for you as a wife?

10. *Do all to the glory of God.*
    Write out 1 Corinthians 10:31 here.

    Now, is the service you are rendering to your husband glorifying to God? Why or why not?

    How can you bring greater glory to God through serving your husband?

11. *Confess any bitterness of heart.*
    Look at Hebrews 12:15 in your Bible. Can you detect any little thoughts or attitudes growing in your heart that could become a root of bitterness?

    Read *The Five "Watches"* again. Which "watch" needs your attention today?

12. *Learn to ask your husband.*

How do think asking your husband (rather than telling him...or announcing a decision *you've* made) shows your respect and regard for him? And what will you do to make this one more "little thing" a permanent thing in your role as a wife? (Just for fun, see how the Shunammite woman asked her husband...before she extended hospitality to the prophet Elisha in 2 Kings 4:8-10!)

13. *Put your husband first, even ahead of yourself.*

Write out Philippians 2:3-4 here, inserting your husband's name each time the verse uses the word "others." (And don't forget to fill in your name in the appropriate places!)

Looking Upward

Please read the "Looking Upward" section in your book again. As you consider the contents of this chapter and God's high calling to you, write out your personal "Prayer for Godly Living."

Chapter Eleven

ssential

A Woman's High Calling to Her Family

"...admonish the young women to
love their chilaren..."
—TITUS 2:4

Begin this lesson by reading chapter 11, "A Woman's High Calling to Her Family," in your personal copy of *A Woman's High Calling*. Note here any new truths or challenges that stand out to you.

Has a "bomb" ever gone off in your home? Can you recall your own "bad home day"? Have you ever needed (or do you need!) to remind yourself of how much you wanted and love your children? Spend a few minutes reflecting, and pinpoint one such incident you could share with your group.

A Look at God's Calling to Love

A reminder—Write out God's high calling from Titus 2:4 to mothers.

And then remember—"Love is the highest blessing in an earthly home, and of this the wife and mother is the natural center." Here are a few godly moms from days gone by— "Mothers Who Made History"—who "remembered" God's high calling upon their lives.

The mother of England's famous William E. Gladstone led her son to faith in God when he was nine. He chose as his life's motto: "In practice, the great thing is that the life of God may be the supreme habit of my soul." He also wrote, "All I think, all I write, all I am is based on the divinity of Jesus Christ, the central hope of our poor wayward race."

Oliver Cromwell's mother taught him the simple truths of Scripture and he chose as his favorite verse, "I can do all things through Christ which strengtheneth me."

The mother of Dwight L. Moody struggled against poverty on a New England farm. A widow with many problems, she taught her son the importance of eternal values. At seventeen, Moody accepted Christ and a few years later dedicated his life for service.[15]

A definition—Which part of the definition in your book meant the most to you...and why?

A decision (or two)—Have you yet made the two decisions below? Write "yes" or "no" and then explain why or why not.

   🔊 *Decision #1*—A decision to be taught Christian mothering by an older Christian woman.

   🔊 *Decision #2*—A decision to teach Christian mothering to younger Christian women.

A Look at God's Teaching

Your assignment here is twofold. First, write out each of these scriptures in the space provided. And second, note anything that was new to you or any new areas for improvement.

   1. Deuteronomy 6:6-7—

   2. Proverbs 1:8—

   3. 1 Timothy 2:15—

   4. Titus 2:3-4—

A Sampling of Loving Mothers

We've talked at length throughout this study (and will continue to do so for nine more chapters!) about the role and responsibility of older women to teach and model God's high callings...and the role and responsibility of younger women to seek out such teaching. But even if you haven't yet found another woman to help you grow in these essentials for godly living, you always have the wonderful women of the Bible who have gone before you. Consider these women (all mothers) from God's Word and the major lesson you can learn from each one. Be sure to write that lesson down and take the time—and space!—to comment on it. For instance, why is the lesson important? What will you do in response to it?

Sarah and others (see pages 163–164 in your book)—

Hannah—

Mary, the mother of Jesus—

Eunice—

Lois—

As you look back over these five major lessons, how can you begin to implement them today...this week...forever...so that the image of Jesus Christ (Lord willing!) can better be stamped upon "the coin of character" in your children?

Looking Upward

Please read the "Looking Upward" section in your book again. As you consider the contents of this chapter and God's high calling to you, write out your personal "Prayer for Godly Living."

Chapter Twelve

Loving Your Family—
An Essential for Godly Living

"...admonish the young women to
love their children..."
—TITUS 2:4

Begin this lesson by reading chapter 12, "Loving Your Children—An Essential for Godly Living," in your personal copy of *A Woman's High Calling*. Note here any new truths or challenges that stand out to you.

I hope you enjoyed the poem about shaping the hearts and minds of your children (and grandchildren)! I also hope you will refer to it often. It truly reminds us of the value of spending the days that we do have with our children, loving them and molding them in godly directions.

Ten Ways to Love Your Children

1. *Teach them*—Write out here these scriptures about the mother's role as a teacher.

Proverbs 1:8—

Proverbs 6:20—

Proverbs 31:1—

Now take a look at your calendar (again!). And glance just at the current month. What kinds of appointments are written there that involve your children? activities? ball games? practices? lessons? meetings? after-school events? entertainment? social gatherings? parties? clubs?

One picture is truly worth a thousand words! Now think through your daily schedule and estimate how much time you spend each day teaching your children the foundational things of the Christian faith and taking them to Christian and church activities, classes, meetings, and so on.

Write out what you discovered, and then write out three major changes you plan to make in the upcoming week. (And don't forget to put them on your calendar...and check here when this is done____.)

Change #1—

Change #2—

Change #3—

2. *Train them*—Copy out these verses directed to Christian parents.

   Proverbs 22:6—

   Ephesians 6:1—

   Describe the kind of training and instruction and parental lessons your children are receiving at their mother's knee. Then write out a few additions you plan to make to the curriculum.

3. *Talk to God about them*—Write out James 5:16 here...and substitute the word "mother" for "man."

   In your lessons about your marriage you (hopefully!) made a prayer page or set up a prayer book for your dear husband. Now do the same for each child. (Check here when this is done_____.)

4. *Talk to them about God*—Look again at Deuteronomy 6:6-7 in your Bible. Then make your plans today for living out the commands in Deuteronomy 6 tomorrow. Plan (and write out here) something to say about God...

   ...when your children get up in the morning—

...when your family eats breakfast—

...and lunch—

...and dinner—

...when your children arrive home after school—

...when you are driving in the car—

...when your children go to bed—

In other words, plan to talk about the Lord. Plan to *take* every opportunity to talk about God. And plan to *make* opportunities to talk about God.

5. *Take time to read on mothering*—Again, whether you are a "reader" or not, you can learn to become a better mother by reading. Talk with your Christian friends to find out about—or make your own list of—three books on mothering.

   Book #1—

   Book #2—

   Book #3—

Now make your own grid or checksheet (or list on your calendar) that will reflect the "little" act of reading just five minutes a day on child-raising. (Check here when this is done_____.)

6. *Take time to read to them*—The older women are to teach the younger ones "good things" (Titus 2:3). And you are to be a teacher of good things to your "younger ones" too. One way this God-given assignment is accomplished is by reading to your family. Does your church have a library? Do your friends have some good Christian books they could loan you to read to your children? Do you need to begin to build a little library for your little ones? Check your Christian bookstore or a Christian book catalog or check with other mothers to help get you started. But whatever you do, take time to read to your children...today! (Check here when this is done_____.)

7. *Teach them to pray*—What did the disciples request of Jesus in Luke 11:1?

Do you pray with your children (no matter what their age)...

...at every meal?	Yes	No	Why not?
...at snack time?	Yes	No	Why not?
...at bedtime?	Yes	No	Why not?
...at family devotions?	Yes	No	Why not?

...when they have a problem?   Yes   No   Why not?

Dear mother, we teach our children to pray by praying with them.

8. *Take care of them*—Write out Proverbs 31:27 here.

How is the "caring quotient" around your house? Look into your heart and into your daily life in regard to providing care through food, clothes, rest, order, a safe place, a schedule, a place of peace, and so on. Is anything missing or offered in a half-hearted, half-done, half-baked way? If so, what do you plan to do about it? (Remember, you are always the primary caregiver when it comes to your children!)

9. *Tell them about Jesus*—Write out Romans 10:14-15 here.

And 2 Timothy 3:15.

You, dear mother, are not only to be a provider...you are to be a "preacher"! It's one thing to teach your children about Noah's ark. But it was Jesus Christ who died for them and who makes it possible for them to have eternal life. What are you actively teaching to enlighten your brood about the Savior's life and death on their behalf?

10. *Try your best (with the Lord's help) to model godliness—*
Write out Proverbs 31:30 here.

And 1 Timothy 2:9-10.

Is there any behavior, conduct, or practice that you need
to eliminate today? (As someone has pointedly warned,
if we don't set aside all ungodliness today, it will more
than likely show up in our children tomorrow!)

Looking Upward

Please read the "Looking Upward" section in your book
again. As you consider the contents of this chapter and
God's high calling to you, write out your personal "Prayer for
Godly Living."

Chapter Thirteen

ssential

A Woman's High Calling to Wisdom

...admonish the young women...
to be discreet..."
—TITUS 2:4-5

Begin this lesson by reading chapter 13, "A Woman's High Calling to Wisdom," in your personal copy of *A Woman's High Calling*. Note here any new truths or challenges that stand out to you.

A Calling to All Christians

As we began this section in your book, I gave you a list of English translations of the word *sophron*—this all-important calling of wisdom upon our lives. Take your English dictionary in hand and jot down a few notes of definition for each of these synonyms:

discreet—

temperate—

self-controlled—

sober—

sober-minded—

sensible—

reasonable—

wise—

orderly—

Can you write out a simple statement that embraces the basic meaning of these words? For instance, did you see any repetition within the definitions? Any actions repeated? A general tone of meaning? Do your best to summarize this calling to be discreet in a few words.

Now take your Bible in hand and look at these scriptures that show us God's calling to wisdom:

elders or overseers—Titus 1:8

older men—Titus 2:2

older women—Titus 2:3

younger women—Titus 2:5

all believers—Titus 2:12

What conclusion(s) can you draw about this calling and its importance to all Christians?

A Calling to Wisdom As a Lifestyle

First, the word—What is the Greek word for wisdom, as presented in your book?

And what areas of your life does it encompass?

What benefits do you think we (and others, beginning with those under our own roof!) would enjoy if our passions and thoughts were under control, if we were self-controlled and of a sound mind?

Next, some meanings—As you read through the words that others have used to define the meaning of our high calling to wisdom and discretion, which ones gave you new information, or made you stop and think, or made you desire this quality more?

Finally, some opposites—Now take your English dictionary in hand and jot down a few notes of definition for these opposites of wisdom and discretion:

foolishness—

rashness—

overenthusiastic—

impulsive—

emotional—

improper—

How would a life characterized by such traits be detrimental to your goal for godly living?

Marks of a Woman of Wisdom

1. *She knows her priorities...and practices them.* The sub-title of your book is "Ten Essentials for Godly Living." All ten are drawn from Titus 2:3-5—use the Contents pages in your book as a quick reference to remind you of them. Try your hand at slotting the ten essentials under the three lifetime goals:

    Goal #1:   We are to cultivate godly conduct and be-havior. Which essentials have to do with godly conduct?

    Goal #2:   We are to cultivate family relationships that honor the Lord. Which essentials have to do with family relationships?

    Goal #3:   We are to cultivate godly character qualities. Which essentials have to do with godly char-acter qualities?

For a look at these three goals lived out in one woman, read Proverbs 31:10-31. Try your hand at making a list of this woman's...

...godly character qualities

...godly relationships

...godly conduct

(Caution—don't make this a laborious project! Just take a careful look at her life.)

Now, how can you keep a more diligent eye...

...on your heart

...on your homefront

...on heaven

How can we develop the right priorities?

Right priorities begin with God—Proverbs 3:5-6. To receive God's guidance, we must acknowledge God in all our ways. This means turning every area of life over to Him. Make Him a vital part of everything you do; then He will guide you because you will be working to accomplish His purposes.

Right priorities grow out of consistent dependence on God—Matthew 6:33. To seek first God's kingdom and His righteousness means to turn to God first for help, to fill your thoughts with His desires, to take His character for your pattern, and to serve and obey Him in everything.

Right priorities grow out of obedience to Christ—Matthew 8:22. Jesus did not hesitate to demand complete loyalty. The decision to follow Jesus should not be put off, even though other loyalties compete for our attention. Nothing should be placed above a total commitment to living for Him.[16]

2. *She is balanced in every area of life.* Are you in search of balance? Beautiful balance? As we finish this lesson, two exercises will help you make headway toward the desirable quality of balance in life. First, look up the scripture given to better your understanding of each of these vital areas. Second, make your own attempt (in your workbook, on paper, on your calendar, or in your personal planner) at balance for the upcoming week.

   Spiritual life—Luke 10:27

Family life—Titus 2:4-5

Home life—Titus 2:5

Church life—1 Corinthians 12:7

Physical life—1 Corinthians 9:27

Social life—Proverbs 18:24 and Luke 10:27

Financial life—Matthew 25:21

Mental life—Romans 15:4 and Psalm 19:14

Looking Upward

Please read the "Looking Upward" section in your book again. As you consider the contents of this chapter and God's high calling to you, write out your personal "Prayer for Godly Living."

Chapter Fourteen

Essential 7

Wisdom—An Essential for Godly Living

"...admonish the young women...
to be discreet..."
—TITUS 2:4-5

 Begin this lesson by reading chapter 14, "Wisdom—An Essential for Godly Living," in your personal copy of *A Woman's High Calling*. Note here any new truths or challenges that stand out to you.

It's time for you to look up Proverbs 11:22 in your Bible. First, write out a description of a pig and its habits. Then describe how ridiculous it would be to have a jeweled nose ring in its snout. What would happen to the jewel? And would that jewel enhance the pig? Why or why not?

Then describe the most physically beautiful woman you can think of. What happens to your image of such a woman when she opens her mouth and speaks loudly, harshly, foolishly, indecently, or cruelly? Or what happens to that lovely image when she acts grossly, in an unfeminine manner, or aggressively?

This powerful exercise shows us the value of wisdom in our lives as women who are called by God to godly living.

Now write out the two marks of a woman of wisdom that we covered in our previous chapter, and then we'll move on to three more marks.

1.

2.

3. *She is farsighted*—How was wisdom defined in this section of your book?

    § Farsightedness will require a decision to *pause*.

        Write out Proverbs 14:30 here. (And for your information—and for clarification—one version of the Bible translates "envy" as "passion": the NASB.)

        As we discovered, your goal is a neutral heart—a heart that is passion-less and can take it or leave it, whatever "it" may be. How do you think *pausing* can help you to gain a neutral heart? To make a wise decision? To walk in a self-controlled manner? To practice personal discipline?

George Mueller of Bristol, England, was an example to all believers of the life of faith, as he trusted God for the care of hundreds of children in his orphanages. His walk with God was also marked by his ability to discern the will of God, "in matters," as he used to say, "both trivial and important."

When asked about this he replied, "I seek at the beginning to get my heart into such a state that it has no will of its own in regard to a given matter. Nine-tenths of the difficulties are overcome when our hearts are ready to do the Lord's will, whatever it may be. When one is in this state, it is usually but a little way to the knowledge of what His will is."[17]

§ Farsightedness will require a decision to pray.

What does James 1:5 teach us about the role of *prayer* in gaining wisdom?

And Philippians 4:6-7?

And Proverbs 1:7?

And Proverbs 9:10?

§ Farsightedness will require a decision to *ponder.*

Can you think of any serious decisions you must make where a decision to *pause, pray,* and *ponder* would help? Write out your dilemma and then complete your thoughts—"If I (<u>do this...or fail to do this,...you fill in the blank</u>), what might happen later...?" (Also be sure you think of scriptures that will guide your decision. Obviously, as a woman looking to answer God's high calling to wisdom, you'll want to follow the guidance of Scripture!) Always take time to think your decisions through *before* you make them. Remember, *wisdom weighs all the options and then makes the right decision.*

4. *She works at wisdom*—Write out Proverbs 4:7 here.

Now read through Proverbs 2:1-5 and make a list of the verbs. This exercise will show you the intense action—work!—on your part that is required to grow in wisdom. Then enjoy one commentator's exhortation regarding these verses.

Verse 1—

Verse 2—

Verse 3—

Verse 4—

Verse 5—

> The first step in getting wisdom is to have motivation or determination. We get in life what we go after. We should get wisdom at all cost, and in the process get good insight and discernment. This means, among other things, that we will learn to choose between the evil and the good, the good and the best, the soulish and the spiritual, the temporal and the eternal.[18]

Here are some other ways to "work" at wisdom...

§ *Spiritually*...We must pray. We've mentioned prayer pages and a prayer book—and prayer!—many times in this book. Take a moment here and now to evaluate your prayer habits. Do they characterize you as a woman who is serious about gaining wisdom? Please explain...and then write out a prescription for bettering your prayer habits.

§ *Mentally*...We must prepare. We've also mentioned preparing for the days and events of life. Again, take a moment here and now to evaluate the use of your mind as you approach each day. Also write out Proverbs 15:14. Into which "mental" category do you fall? Why or why not? Again, do your mental habits characterize you as a woman who is serious about gaining wisdom? Please explain...and then write out a prescription for bettering the use of your mind.

§ *Practically...*We must follow through. Are you a planner and not a doer? Or are you a planner *and* a doer? Write out Proverbs 14:23. How do you measure up? Again, do your practical habits characterize you as a woman who is serious about living life in a wise way and having a life marked by active wisdom, discretion, and sober-mindedness? Please explain...and then write out a prescription for bettering your practice of follow-through.

§ *Educationally...*We must ask for help. Oh, dear one, this is what the book *A Woman's High Calling* is all about! It's about the older women *teaching* the younger women...and the younger women *asking* the older women for their instruction and help. Who is your older woman? Or better yet, do you have a corps of godly older women? And who are the younger women you are assisting as they seek to grow in wisdom? As in the other exercises, write out a prescription to place this essential for godly living in a prominent place in your daily life.

5. *She practices the seven steps of wisdom*—Read Proverbs 1:1-19 for yourself. Jot down here the seven steps of wisdom listed in your book. See if you can pick out these steps in the passage in Proverbs 1. How can they help *you* to keep from running headlong into trouble?

   1.

2.

3.

4.

5.

6.

7.

Looking Upward

Please read the "Looking Upward" section in your book again. As you consider the contents of this chapter and God's high calling to you, write out your personal "Prayer for Godly Living."

Chapter Fifteen

A Woman's High Calling to Purity

"...admonish the young women...
to be chaste..."
—Titus 2:4-5

 Begin this lesson by reading chapter 15, "A Woman's High Calling to Purity," in your personal copy of *A Woman's High Calling*. Note here any new truths or challenges that stand out to you.

Purity As a Calling

Review here the primary teachings presented by the apostle Paul in...

Titus 2:3—

Titus 2:4—

In this study we are seeking to understand God's high callings to us. And we're endeavoring to put into practice (and into our lives!) the essentials that make up godly living. Before we move into the three remaining essentials, let's pause to reflect and evaluate what God is teaching us in these few but powerful verses.

How has your thinking changed about the category Paul labels as "older women"? Do you see it as positive? Does it excite you? Are you owning God's role for your life—either now (if you are "older") or for later? Are you asking God for His help—and "doing the work"—that will make these essentials a permanent part of your life? Are you actively preparing yourself for teaching these essentials to other women? Are you yet involved in assisting the younger women you know to grow in these "good things"? Briefly write out your thinking...or your new thinking.

And how has your thinking changed about the category Paul calls "the young women"? Do you see being a learner as positive? Does it excite you? Are you owning God's role for your life, the role of being a perpetual learner? Are you seeking out and asking older women for help? Are you purposefully seeking knowledge (Proverbs 15:14)? Are you asking God for His help—and "doing the work"—that will put these essentials for godly living into place in your daily life? Briefly write out your thinking...or your new thinking.

Purity Defined

Now it's time to get out your Bible. Look at these scriptures regarding purity and answer the following questions:

    ❧ 1 Peter 3:2—Read verses 1-6 in this chapter. What effect do you think "chaste" conduct has on a husband who is a Christian? On a husband who is *not* a Christian?

    ❧ 1 Timothy 5:22—Here Paul is giving young "Pastor Timothy" some fatherly advice. Why do you think purity was important in the life of this young pastor?

    ❧ 2 Corinthians 11:2—Read verse 3, too. What do you learn here about the mind and purity?

    ❧ Philippians 4:8—What guidelines does Paul give here for your thought life? What kind of thoughts would be "pure"?

    ❧ Titus 2:5—Why do you think purity is important in young women? In young wives? In older women?

§ James 3:17—Describe the wisdom that is from above. Why do you think purity is a mark of godly wisdom?

§ 1 John 3:3—Did you know you play a role in your purity? What does the apostle John say that role is? What steps do you think would help you to accomplish this?

Two Thoughts on Chastity

~ Chastity is to have the body in the soul's keeping. ~
~ Chastity is the most unpopular of Christian virtues.[19] ~

Purity Explained

After reading through this section in your book, write out what you learned about purity and its meaning. Also share what was new to you, what challenged you, and what made purity desirable.

Holiness is not a series of do's and don'ts, but a conformity to God's character in the very depths of our being. This conformity is possible only as we are united with Christ.[20]

Purity...and the Lack Thereof!...Demonstrated

Oh, those women of the Bible! They teach us so many lessons...including lessons about purity!

Dinah—This woman's sad story is told in Genesis 34:1-2. Read it now. What did Dinah do...and what was the consequence of her actions?

What lessons can you draw from Dinah's error?

(If you want to learn the full consequences of Dinah's decision to venture out alone and take a look around, read the rest of Genesis 34...if you can handle it!)

Potiphar's wife—Now read this "bad" woman's story in Genesis 39:1-20. Make a list of her overt and aggressive actions that were anything but chaste and pure. And make it as long as you can! Her words, actions, re-actions, planning, conniving, and accusations are all indicators of a *lack* of purity and chastity!

What harm did this vile woman bring to the righteous Joseph's life?

How did Potiphar's wife live our the definition of sin, that reads...

"Sin is spelled **S**-e-l-f-**I**-s-h-**N**-e-s-s"?

Now for a bonus question—Read through Proverbs 7:6-21, make the same kind of list, and then compare the two lists.

Ruth—Finally, a pure, chaste woman! What do you learn about the sorrow in Ruth's life in Ruth 1:1-5?

And what noble decision did Ruth make in Ruth 1:6-18?

When Ruth was instructed by her mother-in-law to approach their kinsman Boaz as he lay sleeping in the threshing area, what response did Ruth receive from Boaz in Ruth 3:11?

And, to receive a blessing yourself, read Ruth 4:13-22 to see how God blessed Ruth! Just jot down a few.

Mary—Almost everyone knows about the purity of Mary, the mother of Jesus. Indeed, she is known as "the virgin Mary." Read Luke 1:26-38. How is Mary described in verse 27?

And what is Mary's concern in verse 34?

And how did the prophet describe the Messiah in Isaiah 7:14?

Also, how did the angel Gabriel greet Mary in Luke 1:28 and refer to her in verse 30?

We learned earlier that we are to think on what is pure (Philippians 4:8). Read Luke 1:46-55. What do you learn from these verses about Mary's thoughts and heart? Now...what can you do this week to let the Word of Christ dwell in you richly (Colossians 3:16)?

Elizabeth—This cousin of Mary's was also a woman after God's own heart! Her heart and mind were also set on the Lord and on things above. Write out here the description God gives of this wonderful, godly "older"(!) woman in Luke 1:6. What do you think this description reveals about Elizabeth's pure devotion to God?

How might she have responded to her problem of barrenness?

Is there any "problem" in your life that you are allowing to deter you from a pure passion for God and for being a godly woman?

Looking Upward

Please read the "Looking Upward" section in your book again. As you consider the contents of this chapter and God's high calling to you, write out your personal "Prayer for Godly Living."

Chapter Sixteen

Purity—An Essential for Godly Living

"...admonish the young women...
to be chaste..."
—TITUS 2:4-5

Begin this lesson by reading chapter 16, "Purity—An Essential for Godly Living," in your personal copy of *A Woman's High Calling*. Note here any new truths or challenges that stand out to you.

As we move into this practical lesson on purity, consider again the "checklist" for purity:

✓ *Purity is an issue of the heart*—Look at Proverbs 2:11 and 16-19 in your Bible. How did a slip in her heart and in its passion for God possibly set off a chain reaction in this woman's conduct?

Can you detect any such slippage in your heart? Is the temperature of your love for and devotion to God dropping from fervent to indifferent? How can a woman whose heart is set on answering God's high callings to godliness and purity keep a "hot" heart toward the Lord her God?

✓ *Purity is an issue of character*—Can you see the connection between habitual self-restraint and a character marked by purity? Please explain.

✓ *Purity is an issue of the mind*—Read Philippians 4:8 again. How do you think thinking on things that are pure helps keep your soul pure?

And how do you think thinking on things that are pure affects your conduct and choices?

✓ *Purity is an issue of modesty*—Do you agree or disagree that our choice of clothing and conduct reveals the level of our purity? Why or why not?

How Can We Be Pure in Thought?

1. *Use the word No!*—Our chapter mentioned paying careful attention and saying No! to what we think and see that might invite impure thoughts. What does Proverbs 4:23-27 have to say about saying the word "No!"?

2. *Develop a battle plan*—Read these scriptures for yourself and write out any and all commands for action. Especially note the verbs.

   Philippians 4:8 (again!)—

   Colossians 3:1-2—

   Psalm 101:1-4—

   Like David, write out your own set of "I will's" in a vow for a holy life.

3. *Feed on the Word of God*—What question did the psalmist ask in Psalm 119:9...and how did he answer that question in verse 11?

   What role does the Word of God play in our lives, according to the words Jesus prayed in John 17:17?

   List the four benefits of God's Word as named in 2 Timothy 3:16-17.

   —

—

—

—

Hear these thoughts concerning the role of the Word of God in your life—

> True purity comes from God. A follower of Christ becomes sanctified (set apart for sacred use, cleansed and made holy) through believing and obeying the Word of God (Hebrews 4:12)....But daily application of God's Word has a purifying effect on our mind and heart. Scripture points out sin, motivates us to confess, renews our relationship with Christ, and guides us back to the right path.[21]

Now...how important is feeding on God's Word to you? And how does your daily schedule reflect its importance?

4. *Make a radical commitment*—Jesus dealt in the radical! What did He suggest to His listeners in Matthew 5:29 and 39?

Hear again the thoughts of the author above—"True purity comes from radical commitment.... God wants us to be pure. He wants us to clean up our behavior when we begin a new life with him."[22]

Are there any radical commitments you need to make that will help you to answer God's high calling for purity?

If so, be sure that you make them...right now! It's an essential for godly living!

How Can We Be Pure in Word?

What does Proverbs 4:24 say about your speech?

And Proverbs 6:16-19?

And Ephesians 5:3-4?

And James 1:21?

Now, on the more positive side, what solution does 1 Peter 2:1-2 provide?

And Ephesians 4:29?

And Colossians 4:6?

Are there any "radical commitments" you need to make in the area of cleaning up your speech (so to speak!) that will help you to be pure in word? Or put another way, what can you do this week to watch what you say in order to ensure that it is pure?

How Can We Be Pure in Deed?

Read 1 Timothy 2:9-10 in your personal Bible and note these three guidelines for purity in deed found there.

Guideline #1—Modesty. "Modesty," writes one theologian, "refers to a healthy sense of shame at *saying* anything, *doing* anything, or *dressing* in any way that would cause a man to lust" (emphases added).[23] We've already considered the need for our words and speech to be pure. Now let's address our deeds and dress. Read Genesis 38:14-15, Isaiah 3:16-23, and Proverbs 7:10. What statement do these scriptures make about the clothing of women?

Guideline #2—Propriety. How do you think our choice of clothing as Christian women reflects upon God and reflects our regard for God? Also reflect on the end of Titus 2:5.

How do you think women who are and desire to be "reverent in behavior" (Titus 2:3) would and should dress?

Guideline #3—Moderation. There seem to be two extremes in clothing—too much and too little! What was the problem in 1 Timothy 2:9?

Paul's point is that moderation is a key to godly living, to godly conduct, to godly dress. Moderation means not too much...and it means not too little. Can you think of any changes you need to make in any area of your life—more specifically, deeds and dress that would cause a problem for the opposite sex—to follow God's guideline of moderation?

A Picture of Impurity

Look in your own Bible at Proverbs 7 and the description that begins in verse 5. Read it. Mark it well. And make a list of the many unchaste and impure words and deeds of this unchaste woman (and wife!). And then note what a pure and chaste godly woman would do instead.

Ungodly Conduct   Godly Conduct

Looking Upward

Please read the "Looking Upward" section in your book again. As you consider the contents of this chapter and God's high calling to you, write out your personal "Prayer for Godly Living."

Chapter Seventeen

A Woman's High Calling to Her Home

"...admonish the young women... to be homemakers..."
—TITUS 2:4-5

Begin this lesson by reading chapter 17, "A Woman's High Calling to Her Home," in your personal copy of *A Woman's High Calling*. Note here any new truths or challenges that stand out to you.

A Calling (Back!) to Home

As with every calling in Titus 2:3-5, God's high calling to homemaking is a dual calling.

§ The older women are called to *teach* and *admonish* the young women to be homemakers (Titus 2:3-5). What does this calling to teach homemaking assume of the older women?

§ The young women are called to *learn* how to be homemakers (Titus 2:5). What does this calling assume of the attitudes of these young women?

A Calling to Care

We've considered God's instructions to us to be homemakers in Titus 2:3-5. Now look at His calling in 1 Timothy 5:13-14. How were these young women and widows spending their days (verse 13)?

What prescription is given for the ungodly life-pattern that was emerging in these women's lives (verse 14)?

By contrast, how were the older women and widows spending their days, or how had they spent them (verse 10)? Or put another way, how were these godly women answering God's high calling to care for others?

As you consider the definition and meaning of God's calling to us to be homemakers—*oikourgous* (*oikos* meaning the people and place of home, and *ergon* meaning "to do work"), what message is sent straight from God's Word to your heart?

Can you think of three ways you can better care for the people and the place that make up your home?

—

—

—

A Calling to Be Queen (...of the Home)

1. Homemaking is a *priority*. "Home is where the heart is." Is your heart at home? Do you yearn to be there? Do you love to be there? Do you love putting forth the thought, prayer, and effort that turns it from a house into a home? Look at your calendar from last week—your appointments, commitments, meetings, outings, ministries, and outside responsibilities. How much time were you actually at home? Write out a number here to indicate the actual number of hours you spent there (and that doesn't include sleeping!) _____. What changes must you make to make home a higher priority in your heart? (And don't forget to make a schedule that reflects these changes!)

2. Homemaking is a *privilege*. Write out these scriptures here.

   Proverbs 9:1—

   Proverbs 14:1—

   Proverbs 24:3—

   Proverbs 31:27—

   With what attitude do you normally approach your homemaking? Is it as a privilege? Please explain.

3. Homemaking is about *people*. Who are the people who live under your roof? Name them here. (And if you live alone, name those who regularly pass through your doors.) Do these people receive the ministry of your love and loving preparations? Please explain.

4. Homemaking is about a *place*. What do you think these precious people think about the home you are "making"? Or put another way, what do they experience when they come to your home? How are they greeted? What do they see, smell, hear, taste, and sense?

   Take a look at the home of King Solomon and the impression it made on the Queen of Sheba in 1 Kings 10:1-9. What did she see and witness in his home?

   What conclusions did the Queen of Sheba come to regarding the people who lived and served in Solomon's house?

   What conclusions did the Queen of Sheba come to regarding the source of such a place?

A Fireplace Motto
The beauty of the house is order;
The blessing of the house is contentment;
The glory of the house is hospitality;
The crown of the house is godliness.[24]

5. Homemaking is a *passion*—not a prison. Write out Proverbs 31:13 here—

And Proverbs 31:27 (again!)—

And Ecclesiastes 9:10—

Take the temperature of your emotional fervor and passion for your home and for the people there. Would you rate your feelings and emotions about home and homemaking as a passion? Why or why not? And what can you do to turn up the heat of your passion toward home? Now, what *will* you do?

6. Homemaking is a *profession*. What a blessing older women are to younger ones when they take their homemaking seriously, approach it as a profession, and then turn around and pass it on! Are you preparing to pass on what you are learning about the profession of homemaking? Do you see homemaking as a profession? Why or why not?

7. Homemaking is a matter for *prayer*. We've already made pages for our husband and children in our prayer books. Now make a page for your homemaking. Better yet, make 20 pages:

One page—for attitudes to pray for and scriptures to pray over. (This list from your book of ten terms that describe godly homemaking for us would make a nice start. And the many scriptures we're applying.)

Seven pages—for the days of the week. You'll want to divide up your good-housekeeping chores into the seven days of the week.

Twelve pages—for the months of the year. For instance, May is very special around our house— that's when we celebrate Jim's birthday and Katherine's birthday, and now her husband Paul has been added to the May list. Plus you know what November and December mean! And then there's that thing called "spring cleaning." Every month brings with it special opportunities for special projects that involve special people and the special place called home.

Place these pages in your prayer notebook to be looked over, worked over, and prayed over daily. I promise you, such pages will transform your house *work* into something truly exciting! (Check here when this is done_____.)

8. Homemaking is *permanent*. Where does the Lord have you today, dear one? Wherever it is (a hotel room, a dorm room, a mobile home, a rented apartment, a palatial home with servants, a foreign country, a boat), you are the homemaker, and that place is yours to "make." It's your high calling from God. What one thing can you do right this minute that would "make" it a better place, a place that would better minister to people, a place that would better glorify God?

9. Homemaking sets a *pattern*. One Christian song expresses this well—that those who come behind us may find us faithful. Just think, others *will* "come behind us." That means we are setting the pattern for those others to follow. Now, who are the "others" in your life, the young women and girls in your life? What are you doing to set the pattern for them, the time-honored and godly pattern of homemaking? And will they find that you were faithful to your God-given assignment to "make" your house a home?

10. Homemaking is a *practice*—and is to be practiced. Practice leads to perfection. And homemaking is an art that, like all arts, is made up of skills. Are there any skills you need to learn or better learn? If so, who can help you and what can you do to better practice this noble art?

Looking Upward

Please read the "Looking Upward" section in your book again. As you consider the contents of this chapter and God's high calling to you, write out your personal "Prayer for Godly Living."

Chapter Eighteen

Essential

9

Homemaking—An Essential for Godly Living

"...admonish the young women...
to be homemakers..."
—Titus 2:4-5

Begin this lesson by reading chapter 10, "Homemaking—An Essential for Godly Living," in your personal copy of *A Woman's High Calling*. Note here any new truths or challenges that stand out to you.

Home Is Where Your Heart Is

Were you blessed by the description written by Elizabeth Prentiss of her dear Aunty? It portrayed, through the eyes of a teenager, much of what we've been learning in our chapters on marriage, family, and homemaking. But let's get to the "heart" of homemaking—your heart!

1. *Be there.* In our previous study you counted up the hours you are actually at home. A favorite verse of mine reminds us that "Wisdom is in the sight of him who has

understanding, but the eyes of a fool are on the ends of the earth" (Proverbs 17:24). Basically, this verse is telling you and me that the *wise woman* focuses on what is right in front of her, right between her own two feet, right in front of her own two eyes—her home. But the *foolish woman* is looking elsewhere for fulfillment, spending her time elsewhere, thinking that the important things in life are "out there"—anywhere but home! What did you do after our last lesson about increasing the number of hours you are at home? Please write down a few new blessings you, your family, and your home are enjoying as a result.

2. *Pray*. Write out these two verses that put zip and zest—and God's perspective—into our homemaking.

    1 Corinthians 10:31—

    Colossians 3:23—

    How does prayer put these two principles to work in your homemaking?

3. *Devote 30 minutes a day to some kind of home improvement*. Little things add up to a lot! Take your calendar in hand and schedule 30 minutes per day this week, Monday through Saturday, for home improvements. For instance, begin by laying out a towel on your kitchen counter. One by one, turn each of your kitchen drawers

upside down on the towel, sponge it out, and put the items back into the drawer (using a liberal hand to throw away or give away the odd, unused things!). In 30 minutes you should have a kitchen full of clean drawers. Be prepared to share your six projects with your group.

4. *Spend time with women who do love and "make" their homes.* That's the teaching in Titus 2:3-5. Who are the women who continually encourage you in your home-making? And are you becoming such a woman to others?

5. *Invest in something that sparks your interest in your home.* We "make" our homes by loving our homes. And there's no reason we shouldn't do the things we love to do—like special projects or hobbies that better our home-sweet-home. What will that thing be for you this week? Write it on your calendar.

Home Is the Hub

Have you heard about the life of Susannah Wesley? This famous mom (and we've already mentioned her in our book) was not only the mother of John and Charles Wesley, but the mother of 17 other children as well! Can you imagine the hubbub in that godly home? Can you think of a home filled with such happy activity? And more than that, are *you* the "maker" of such a home, a woman like Elizabeth Prentiss's Aunty, a woman who possesses "unflagging good humor and cheerfulness," a woman "full of fun and energy, flying about the house on wings," a woman who creates a center where her family gathers for good times and the ministry of the home? Please explain your answers...and make a few plans for making the hub more of a magnet.

Home Is a Haven

Would you describe your home as a haven? Is it a place where your family members are safe, not only from those outside, but also from those within, from one another? What changes need to occur...and what will you do to implement those changes?

Home Is a Hospital

Would you describe your home as a hospital? Do your loved ones find an environment that ministers to them in the physical requirements of life? And in the emotional area? What changes need to occur...and what will you do to implement those changes?

Home Is to Be Happy

Do you find this general principle to be true in your home—if you are happy, then the members of your family tend to be happy? Write out these scriptures:

Nehemiah 8:10—

Galatians 5:22—

What is to be the source of your joy, dear one? And are you remembering to find your joy in Him? Is there anything you need to do to spread the joy of the Lord to those at home? Note two or three ways to do just that.

Home Is a Hearth

Is the atmosphere in your home a "warm" one, like those of the past where family gathered around the hearth at home for camaraderie? Please explain your answer. For instance, is there a gathering place for the family? And are there gathering times? Or...does each family member have his or her own room, equipped with his or her own TV, telephone, and music? Do any changes need to occur? If so what...and when?

Home Is for Hospitality

First write out one of God's guidelines for hospitality—
1 Peter 4:9.

Then look at these dear women of the Bible who followed this guideline. Make a note here of how each lady extended hospitality.

The widow of Zarephath—1 Kings 17:10-16

The Shunammite woman—2 Kings 4:8-11

Mary, the mother of John Mark—Acts 12:11-17

Lydia—Acts 16:13-15,40

Priscilla and her husband—1 Corinthians 16:19

How does your family practice hospitality? And how can you instill this gracious Christian practice in your children? Answer these questions, and then relish this poem which "wraps up" what a Christian home is.

What Is a Christian Home?

Where family prayer is daily said,
God's Word is regularly read,
And faith in Christ is never dead,
That is a Christian home.

Where family quarrels are pushed aside
To let the love of God abide
Ere darkness falls on eventide,
That is a Christian home.

Where joy and happiness prevail
In every heart without a fail
And thoughts to God on high set sail,
That is a Christian home.

Where Jesus Christ is Host and Guest,
Through whom we have eternal rest
And in Him are forever blest,
That is a Christian home.[25]

Looking Upward

Please read the "Looking Upward" section in your book again. As you consider the contents of this chapter and God's high calling to you, write out your personal "Prayer for Godly Living."

Chapter Nineteen

A Woman's High Calling to Goodness

*"...admonish the young women...
to be good..."*
—TITUS 2:4–5

 Begin this lesson by reading chapter 19, "A Woman's High Calling to Goodness," in your personal copy of *A Woman's High Calling*. Note here any new truths or challenges that stand out to you.

Who...Is to Be Good?

Note the teaching about kindness and goodness in these scriptures:

§ Ephesians 2:10 and Titus 3:1—What is one assignment for every Christian?

§ Galatians 5:16,22-23—How is your walk with God?

§ Titus 2:3,5—What is God's assignment to His older women?

And to His younger women?

§ Acts 9:36-39—How is Dorcas described, and what did she do to merit such words?

Are you challenged in any special way to greater goodness? How and why?

~

*Goodness consists not in the outward things we do,
but in the inward thing we are.*

~

What...Does It Mean to Be Good?

Write out the definition for goodness given in your book.

§ The Proverbs 31 woman was good and kind. How was her goodness extended, according to Proverbs 31:12 and 26?

§   What did the man Job do (and not do!) to qualify in this area of goodness (Job 1:1)?

Where...Is Goodness to Occur?

Read again the text set apart (see page 268 of your book) that describes many "little things" that are good and kind. Now add your own thoughts to that list. Then treat yourself to the definition of goodness as stated by a poet.

> "What is real good?" I asked in a musing mood:
> *Order,* said the law court; *knowledge,* said the school;
> *Truth,* said the wise man; *pleasure,* said the fool;
> *Love,* said the maiden; *beauty,* said the page;
> *Freedom,* said the dreamer; *home,* said the sage;
> *Fame,* said the soldier; *equity,* said the seer—
> Spake my heart full sadly: "The answer is not here";
> Then, within my bosom, softly, this I heard:
> "Each heart holds the secret—*Kindness* is the word."[26]

When...Are We to Be Good?

In a word, to quote John Wesley, when are we to be good?

Can you pinpoint any specific time of day when you need to remember to be good? And how will you remember and prepare for goodness at that time?

Why...Are We to Be Good?

1. *Because kindness and goodness is commanded.* What is the command to Christians in Galatians 6:10?

   (And what word of encouragement is given in Galatians 6:9?)

   What is the command of Ephesians 4:32?

2. *Because kindness and goodness is what a godly woman is all about.* Once again, what are the older women to teach—Titus 2:3?

   And what are the younger women to learn—Titus 2:5?

   How did the women in 1 Timothy 5:10 live out kindness and goodness?

3. *Because kindness and goodness blesses our husband and children.* Read Proverbs 31:10-31 and count the ways this wife and mother blessed her family with deeds of kindness and goodness. Jot down a list.

4. *Because kindness and goodness blesses our home.* And also list the ways the Proverbs 31 woman's good deeds blessed her home.

5. *Because kindness and goodness brings honor to God.* The final words of Titus 2:5 point out the significance of heeding all of God's high callings. What happens when we fail to follow through on the essentials listed in verses 3-5?

Therefore, what happens when we *do* follow through on these ten essentials for godly living?

Now, dear one, what kind of "advertisement" for the gospel of Jesus Christ is your conduct making? After you answer, "wonder" along with this gentleman!

> Several years ago a group of salesmen went to a regional sales meeting in Chicago. They assured their wives that they would be home in plenty of time for supper on Friday night.
>
> One thing led to another and the meeting ran overtime. The men had to race to the airport, tickets in hand. As they barged through the terminal, one man inadvertently kicked over a table supporting a basket of apples. Without stopping they all reached the plane in time and boarded it with a sigh of relief. All but one. He paused...and experienced a twinge

of compassion for the girl whose apple stand had been overturned. He waved good-bye to his companions and returned to the terminal. He was glad he did. The ten-year-old girl was blind.

The salesman gathered up the apples and noticed that several of the apples were battered and bruised. He reached into his wallet and said to the girl, "Here, please take this ten dollars for the damage we did. I hope it didn't spoil your day."

As the salesman started to walk away, the bewildered girl called out to him, "Are you Jesus?"

He stopped in mid-stride...and he wondered.[27]

Looking Upward

Please read the "Looking Upward" section in your book again. As you consider the contents of this chapter and God's high calling to you, write out your personal "Prayer for Godly Living."

Chapter Twenty

Goodness—An Essential for Godly Living

*"...admonish the young women...
to be good"*
—Titus 2:4–5

Begin this lesson by reading chapter 20, "Goodness—An Essential for Godly Living," in your personal copy of *A Woman's High Calling*. Note here any new truths or challenges that stand out to you.

Read Luke 10:38-42 in your own Bible. I'm sure you can relate to dear Martha's absorption in her "dinner party" preparations and her hostessing. Can you think of a time when you fell into Martha's pattern of doing a good work...without the goodness? Or do you have daily work to do in your home that you can do without a heart of goodness if you're not careful? Share about such a time here.

As one commentator remarked, "While performing their tasks in the family...women must take care that the constant strain of domestic duties does not make them irritable or cruel. They must pray for grace to remain kind..to husbands and children."[28]

Why...Are We to Be Good?

Look back over chapter 19 in your book and again at the lesson from your *Growth and Study Guide* for chapter 19. List here the five reasons we are to be good—and then we'll move on to *how* we are to be good.

1.

2.

3.

4.

5.

How...Are We to Be Good?

It's one thing to know *what* we are supposed to do, and even *why*, but knowing *how* is also essential.

1. *Prepare your heart for goodness.* For an exposure to pure goodness, read Psalm 19:7-9 for yourself. How do you think daily exposure to such a "good thing" as the Word of God would change things around your house? Write out your answer, and then see what someone else learned about the difference preparing the heart for the day makes!

The Difference

I got up early one morning
And rushed right into the day;
I had so much to accomplish
That I didn't take time to pray.

Problems just tumbled about me,
And heavier came each task;
"Why doesn't God help me?" I wondered.
He answered: "You didn't ask."

I wanted to see joy and beauty—
But the day toiled on, gray and bleak;
I wondered why God didn't show me.
He said: "But you didn't seek."

I tried to come into God's presence,
I used all my keys at the lock;
God gently and lovingly chided:
"My child, you didn't knock."

I woke up early this morning
And paused before entering the day;
I had so much to accomplish
That I had to take time to pray.[29]

2. *Pray for kindness and goodness.* And while you are preparing your heart with the good things in God's Word, be specific and pray for kindness and goodness. How do you think praying "for greater love and compassion for others" would make a difference in your heart of goodness? In your relationships at home? In your many "good" housekeeping chores? In the tone of your home? In kind deeds extended to others? This is important, so take your time.

3. *Plan for kindness.* Take paper in hand and list your husband's and each child's names. Then beside each name, note at least one deed of kindness you can do for each of these precious family members. Next, pick a specific day on your calendar this week and put these deeds into specific time slots on your daily schedule. And of course, finally, act on your plan for kindness! Check off each exercise:

   _____ List your family members

   _____ List possible deeds of kindness for each family member

   _____ Schedule the day and time for each deed of kindness

   _____ Do the deeds of kindness

   _____ Repeat this exercise for the next week

4. *Pore over the life of Christ.* As Peter preached in Acts 10:38, Jesus "went about doing good." Just for today, set aside five minutes and read Mark 1 in your Bible. Make a list (you may want to use a separate sheet of paper) of the many good things Jesus did...in just this one chapter! (Check here when this is done_____.)

   Bonus exercise—Set aside five minutes per day for three months, and each day read just one chapter of the Gospels—Matthew, Mark, Luke, John. Make a list (you'll need a little notebook or journal or notebook paper) of the many good things Jesus went about doing. You'll be astounded...and you'll be changed.

5. *Peruse the women of the Bible.* We've considered many of the women of the Bible in our study of *A Woman's High Calling*. And I'm sure you're aware of more of these gracious, "good" women than we've covered. Think now of your favorite women of the Bible. More specifically, think of those who were good and kind and did the deeds of goodness and kindness. Who are they...and what did they do that evidenced a heart of goodness? Plan to share the blessing of this exercise with those in your study. (And, of course, put their life lessons to practice in your life!)

6. *Put away all that is not kind and good.* In your own words, what does it mean to "put away" what is ungodly?

   Now list what God calls us to "put away" in Colossians 3:5-9.

I'm sure you can see immediately that not one of these behaviors and deeds is good! So...what must be eliminated—put away—from your life so that you can do the better work of putting on what is pleasing to God?

7. *Put on a heart of kindness*. Read Colossians 3:12 for yourself. This is willful, dear one. We must think about kindness and goodness. We must pray for it. We must desire it. We must plan for it. But in the end, with God's help, we must *do* it. In fact, Benjamin Franklin made goodness a daily rule for his life—each day he asked himself, "What good thing can I do today?" Why not ask this question...and answer it...and do one good thing today? (Check here when your good deed is done_____.)

> To do evil for good is human corruption;
> To do good for good is civil retribution;
> But to do good for evil is Christian perfection.
> Though this be not the grace of nature,
> It is the nature of grace.[30]

Why...Are We to Seek the Ten Essentials for Godly Living?

Read the end of Titus 2:5 again. This "purpose clause" applies to all ten of the essentials for godly living that God calls us to. What does Titus 2:5 say is the all-important "why" when it comes to our obedience in these ten essentials? Or put another way, "why" should we set about to answer these high callings from God?

As we come to the end of our wonderful study of *A Woman's High Calling* and the ten essentials that make up that high calling to godly living, let's close with a few of Paul's final words to his friend Titus:

> This is a faithful saying, and these things I want you to affirm constantly, that those who have believed in God should be careful to maintain good works. These things are good and profitable to men [and women].
>
> —TITUS 3:8

Looking Upward

Please read the "Looking Upward" section in your book again. As you consider the contents of this chapter and God's high calling to you, write out your personal "Prayer for Godly Living."

Leading a Bible Study Discussion Group

What a privilege it is to lead a Bible study! And what joy and excitement await you as you delve into the Word of God and help others to discover its life-changing truths. If God has called you to lead a Bible study group, I know you'll be spending much time in prayer and planning and giving much thought to being an effective leader. I also know that taking the time to read through the following tips will help you to navigate the challenges of leading a Bible study discussion group and enjoy the effort and opportunity.

The Leader's Roles

As a Bible study group leader, you'll find your role changing back and forth from *expert* to *cheerleader* to *lover* to *referee* during the course of a session.

Since you're the leader, group members will look to you to be the *expert* guiding them through the material. So be well prepared. In fact, be overprepared so that you know the material better than any group member does. Start your study early in the week, and let its message simmer all week long. (You might even work several lessons ahead so that you have in mind the big picture and the overall direction of the study.) Be ready to share some additional gems that your group members wouldn't have discovered on their own. That extra insight from your study time—or that comment from a wise Bible teacher or scholar, that clever saying, that keen observation from another believer, and even an appropriate joke—adds an element of fun and keeps Bible study from becoming routine, monotonous, and dry.

Second, be ready to be the group's *cheerleader.* Your energy and enthusiasm for the task at hand can be contagious. It can also stimulate people to get more involved in their personal study as well as in the group discussion.

Third, be the *lover,* the one who shows a genuine concern for the members of the group. You're the one who will establish the atmosphere of the group. If you laugh and have fun, the group members will laugh and have fun. If you hug, they will hug. If you care, they will care. If you share, they will share. If you love, they will love. So pray every day to love the women God has placed in your group. Ask Him to show you how to love them with His love.

Finally, as the leader, you'll need to be the *referee* on occasion. That means making sure everyone has an equal opportunity to speak. That's easier to do when you operate under the assumption that very member of the group has something worthwhile to contribute. So, trusting that the Lord has taught each person during the week, act on that assumption.

Expert, cheerleader, lover, and referee—these four roles of the leader may make the task seem overwhelming. But that's not bad if it keeps you on your knees praying for your group.

A Good Start

Beginning on time, greeting people warmly, and opening in prayer gets the study off to a good start. Know what you want to have happen during your time together, and make sure those things get done. That kind of order means comfort for those involved.

Establish a format and let the group members know what that format is. People appreciate being in a Bible study that focuses on the Bible. So keep the discussion on the topic and move the group through the questions. Tangents are often hard to avoid—and even harder to rein in. So be sure to focus on the answers to questions about the specific passage at hand. After all, the purpose of the group is Bible study!

Finally, as someone has accurately observed, "Personal growth is one of the by-products of any effective small group. This growth is achieved when people are recognized and accepted by others. The more friendliness, mutual trust, respect, and warmth exhibited, the more likely that the member will find pleasure in the group, and, too, the more likely she will work hard toward the accomplishment of the group's goals. The effective leader will strive to reinforce desirable traits" (source unknown).

A Dozen Helpful Tips

Here is a list of helpful suggestions for leading a Bible study discussion group:

1. Arrive early, ready to focus fully on others and give of yourself. If you have to do any last-minute preparation, review, re-grouping, or praying, do it in the car. Don't dash in, breathless, harried, late, still tweaking your plans.

2. Check out your meeting place in advance. Do you have everything you need—tables, enough chairs, a blackboard, hymnals if you plan to sing, coffee, and so on?

3. Greet each person warmly by name as she arrives. After all, you've been praying for these women all week long, so let each VIP know that you're glad she's arrived.

4. Use name tags for at least the first two or three weeks.

5. Start on time no matter what—even if only one person is there!

6. Develop a pleasant but firm opening statement. You might say, "This lesson was great! Let's get started so we can enjoy all of it!" or "Let's pray before we begin our lesson."

7. Read the questions, but don't hesitate to reword them on occasion. Rather than reading an entire paragraph of instructions, for instance, you might say, "Question 1 asks us to list some ways that Christ displayed humility. Lisa, please share one way Christ displayed humility."

8. Summarize or paraphrase the answers given. Doing so will keep the discussion focused on the topic, eliminate digressions, help avoid or clear up any misunderstandings of the text, and keep each group member aware of what the others are saying.

9. Keep moving, and don't add any of your own questions to the discussion time. It's important to get through the study guide questions. So if a cut-and-dried answer is called for, you don't need to comment with anything other than a "thank you." But when the question asks for an opinion or an application (for instance, "How can this truth help us in our marriages?" or "How do *you* find time for your quiet time?"), let all who want to contribute.

10. Affirm each person who contributes, especially if the contribution was very personal, painful to share, or a rare statement from a quiet person. Make everyone who shares a hero by saying something like, "Thank you for sharing that insight from your own life" or, "We certainly appreciate what God has taught you. Thank you for letting us in on it."

11. Watch your watch, put a clock right in front of you, or consider using a timer. Pace the discussion so that you meet your cut-off time, especially if you want time to

pray. Stop at the designated time even if you haven't finished the lesson. Remember that everyone has worked through the study once; you are simply going over it again.

12. End on time. You can only make friends with your group members by ending on time or even a little early! Besides, members of your group have the next item on their agenda to attend to—picking up children from the nursery, babysitter, or school; heading home to tend to matters there; running errands; getting to bed; or spending some time with their husbands. So let them out *on time!*

Five Common Problems

In any group, you can anticipate certain problems. Here are some common ones that can arise, along with helpful solutions:

1. *The incomplete lesson*—Right from the start, establish the policy that if someone has not done the lesson, it is best for her not to answer the questions. But do try to include her responses to questions that ask for opinions or experiences. Everyone can share some thoughts in reply to a question like, "Reflect on what you know about both athletic and spiritual training and then share what you consider to be the essential elements of training oneself in godliness."

2. *The gossip*—The Bible clearly states that gossiping is wrong, so you don't want to allow it in your group. Set a high and strict standard by saying, "I am not comfortable with this conversation," or "We [not *you*] are gossiping, ladies. Let's move on."

3. *The talkative member*—Here are three scenarios and some possible solutions for each.

   a. The problem talker may be talking because she has done her homework and is excited about something she has to share. She may also know more about the subject than the others and, if you cut her off, the rest of the group may suffer.

   SOLUTION: Respond with a comment like: "Sarah, you are making very valuable contributions. Let's see if we can get some reactions from the others," or "I know Sarah can answer this. She's really done her homework. How about some of the rest of you?"

   b. The talkative member may be talking because she has *not* done her homework and wants to contribute, but she has no boundaries.

   SOLUTION: Establish at the first meeting that those who have not done the lesson do not contribute except on opinion or application questions. You may need to repeat this guideline at the beginning of each session.

   c. The talkative member may want to be heard whether or not she has anything worthwhile to contribute.

   SOLUTION: After subtle reminders, be more direct, saying, "Betty, I know you would like to share your ideas, but let's give others a chance. I'll call on you later."

4. *The quiet member*—Here are two scenarios and possible solutions for each.

   a. The quiet member wants the floor but somehow can't get the chance to share.

   SOLUTION: Clear the path for the quiet member by first watching for clues that she wants to speak (moving to the edge of her seat, looking as if she wants to speak, perhaps even starting to say something) and then saying, "Just a second. I think Chris wants to say something." Then, of course, make her a hero!

b. The quiet member simply doesn't want the floor.

SOLUTION: "Chris, what answer do you have on question 2?" or "Chris, what do you think about …?" Usually after a shy person has contributed a few times, she will become more confident and more ready to share. Your role is to provide an opportunity where there is *no* risk of a wrong answer. But occasionally a group member will tell you that she would rather not be called on. Honor her request, but from time to time ask her privately if she feels ready to contribute to the group discussions.

In fact, give all your group members the right to pass. During your first meeting, explain that any time a group member does not care to share an answer, she may simply say, "I pass." You'll want to repeat this policy at the beginning of every group session.

5. *The wrong answer*—Never tell a group member that she has given a wrong answer, but at the same time never let a wrong answer go by.

SOLUTION: Either ask if someone else has a different answer, or ask additional questions that will cause the right answer to emerge. As the women get closer to the right answer, say, "We're getting warmer! Keep thinking! We're almost there!"

Learning from Experience

Immediately after each Bible study session, evaluate the group discussion time. You may also want a member of your group (or an assistant or trainee or outside observer) to evaluate you periodically.

Notes

1. Elizabeth George, *A Woman's High Calling* (Eugene, OR: Harvest House Publishers, 2001), p. 194.

2. John Brown, *Expository Discourses on 1 Peter,* as quoted in Charles R. Swindoll, *The Tale of the Tardy Oxcart* (Nashville: Word Publishing, Inc., 1998), p. 268.

3. Elizabeth George, *Loving God with All Your Mind* (Eugene, OR: Harvest House Publishers, 1994), p. 63.

4. Eugene Peterson, *A Long Obedience in the Same Direction*, as quoted in Swindoll, *The Tale of the Tardy Oxcart*, p. 268.

5. Hinton, as quoted in Eleanor L. Doan, ed., *The Speaker's Sourcebook* (Grand Rapids, MI: Zondervan Publishing House, 1977), p. 125.

6. Frank M. Garafda, as quoted in Roy B. Zuck, *The Speaker's Quote Book* (Grand Rapids, MI: Kregel Publications, 1997).

7. Gene A. Getz, as quoted in Elizabeth George, *Growing in Wisdom & Faith—James*, (Eugene, OR: Harvest House Publishers, 2001), p. 89.

8. Getz, as quoted in George, *Growing in Wisdom & Faith,* pp. 92-93.

9. Doan, *The Speaker's Sourcebook*, p. 175.

10. *God's Treasury of Virtues* (Tulsa, OK: Honor Books, Inc., 1995), p. 438.

11. D. L. Moody, *Notes from My Bible and Thoughts from My Library* (Grand Rapids, MI: Baker Book House, 1979), pp. 89-90.

12. William Barclay, *The Letter to the Hebrews*, as quoted in Swindoll, *The Tale of the Tardy Oxcart*, p. 179.

13. Adapted for women in Elizabeth George, *Woman to Woman—Discipling One Another* (Call 1-800-542-4611 or write to Elizabeth George at PO Box 2879, Belfair, WA 98528 to order this notebook and two tapes on mentoring.)

14. Mignon McLaughlin, as quoted in Zuck, *The Speaker's Quote Book*, p. 242.

15. McLaughlin, as quoted in Zuck, *The Speaker's Quote Book,* p. 263.

16. Drawn from Neil S. Wilson, ed., *The Handbook of Bible Application* (Wheaton, IL: Tyndale House Publishers, Inc., 1992), pp. 494-95.

17. Zuck, *The Speaker's Quote Book*, p. 410.

18. William MacDonald, *Enjoying the Proverbs* (Kansas City, KS: Walterick Publishers, 1982), p. 29.

19. Albert M. Wells Jr., ed., *Inspiring Quotations—Contemporary & Classical* (Nashville: Thomas Nelson Publishers, 1988), p. 25.

20. Jerry Bridges, as quoted in *Inspiring Quotations*, p. 88.

21. Wilson, ed., *The Handbook of Bible Application*, pp. 506-507.

22. Wilson, ed., *The Handbook of Bible Application,* p. 506.

23. John MacArthur Jr., *The MacArthur New Testament Commentary—Titus* (Chicago: Moody Press, 1996), p. 85.

24. Frank S. Mead, ed., *12,000 Religious Quotations* (Grand Rapids, MI: Baker Book House, 1989), p. 229.

25. Unknown source, as quoted in Zuck, *The Speaker's Quote Book*, p. 195.

26. John Boyle O'Reilly, as quoted in *God's Treasury of Virtues*, p. 207.

27. Michel Hodgin, *1001 More Humorous Illustrations for Public Speaking* (Grand Rapids, MI: Zondervan Publishing House, 1998), p. 181.

28. William Hendricksen, *New Testament Commentary—The Pastoral Epistles* (Grand Rapids, MI: Baker Book House, 1976), p. 365.

29. Doan, *The Speaker's Sourcebook*, p. 198.

30. William Secker, as quoted in William J. Petersen and Randy Petersen, *The One Year Book of Psalms* (Wheaton, IL: Tyndale House Publishers, Inc., 1999), January 10.

Personal Notes

About the Author

Elizabeth George is a bestselling author and speaker whose passion is to teach the Bible in a way that changes women's lives. For information about Elizabeth's books or speaking ministry, to sign up for her mailings, or to share how God has used this book in your life, please write to Elizabeth at:

Elizabeth George
P.O. Box 2879
Belfair, WA 98528

Toll-free fax/phone: 1-800-542-4611
www.elizabethgeorge.com

Books by Elizabeth George

Beautiful in God's Eyes—The Treasures of the Proverbs 31 Woman
God Lights My Path—Meditations
The Lord Is My Shepherd—12 Promises for Every Woman
Loving God with All Your Mind
A Woman After God's Own Heart®
A Woman After God's Own Heart™ Audiobook
A Woman After God's Own Heart® Growth & Study Guide
A Woman After God's Own Heart® Prayer Journal
Women Who Loved God—365 Days with the Women of the Bible
A Woman's High Calling—10 Essentials for Godly Living
A Woman's High Calling Growth & Study Guide
A Woman's Walk with God—Growing in the Fruit of the Spirit
A Woman's Walk with God Growth & Study Guide

A Woman After God's Own Heart® Bible Study Series
Walking in God's Promises—The Life of Sarah
Cultivating a Life of Character—Judges/Ruth
Becoming a Woman of Beauty & Strength—Esther
Nurturing a Heart of Humility—The Life of Mary
Experiencing God's Peace—Philippians
Pursuing Godliness—1 Timothy
Growing in Wisdom & Faith—James
Putting On a Gentle & Quiet Spirit—1 Peter

Children's Books
God's Wisdom for Little Girls—Virtues & Fun from Proverbs 31
God's Little Girl Is Helpful
God's Little Girl Is Kind